Chesapeake Bay Odyssey

Chesapeake Bay Odyssey:

23 Ports of Call
with
Historic Perspectives

by
Captain Michael J. Dodd

SEAWORTHY PUBLICATIONS, INC.   •   MELBOURNE, FLORIDA

Chesapeake Bay Odyssey:
23 Ports of Call with Historic Perspectives

Copyright © 2022 by Captain Michael J. Dodd

ISBN 978-1-948494-55-7
Any photos or reproductions not credited are those of the author.
Published in the USA by:
Seaworthy Publications, Inc.
6300 N. Wickham Rd., 130-416
Melbourne, Florida 32940
Phone: 310-610-3634
email: orders@seaworthy.com
www.seaworthy.com

Our special thanks to the Williams & Heintz Map Corporation, publishers of the Maryland & Delaware, and Virginia Cruising Guides to the Chesapeake Bay, for allowing us to reprint their maps of the Chesapeake Bay.

Library of Congress Cataloging-in-Publication Data

Names: Dodd, Michael J., 1946- author.
Title: Chesapeake Bay odyssey : 23 ports of call with historic perspectives / by Captain Michael J. Dodd.
Description: Melbourne, Florida : Seaworthy Publications, Inc., [2021] | Includes bibliographical references. | Summary: "The author, Captain Michael Dodd, grew up in Baltimore and spent many hours on the Chesapeake Bay throughout most of his life. His book outlines a fascinating exploration of 23 cities and towns on the Bay from a waterborne perspective. He and his wife, Maureen, motored the length of the Bay during the Covid year of 2020. This book describes their journey, and each chapter starts with a delightful historic outline of the port visited. Little tidbits of tantalizing facts are discovered and explored and make this book more than a simple travelogue. Who knew there was a German U-boat at the bottom of the Potomac River? Or that tiny Tangier Island, Virginia, in the central Bay, was a British resupply fort during the War of 1812? We all know that Francis Scott Key wrote the "Star Bangled Banner" while observing the bombardment of Ft. McHenry in Baltimore. But did you know that he was a temporary captive on a British ship when he watched the event unfold? The author's easy writing style makes this book attractive not only to yachtsmen and boaters of all stripes but to anyone with an interest in American history. This book includes: 23 ports of call Detailed sights to see and historic places to visit Describes entrance to each port Offers suggestions for restaurants and shopping spots Overnight visits to each port-with extra nights at Baltimore, Annapolis, Washington DC, Yorktown, and St. Michaels Suggestions for marinas Offers a summary of Bay historic events and their relationship to world history"-- Provided by publisher.
Identifiers: LCCN 2021027736 (print) | LCCN 2021027737 (ebook) | ISBN 9781948494557 (paperback) | ISBN 9781948494564 (epub)
Subjects: LCSH: Sailing--Chesapeake Bay (Md. and Va.)--Guidebooks. | Chesapeake Bay Region (Md. and Va.)--Description and travel. | Chesapeake Bay Region (Md. and Va.)--Guidebooks.
Classification: LCC F187.C5 D65 2021 (print) | LCC F187.C5 (ebook) | DDC 917.55/18--dc23
LC record available at https://lccn.loc.gov/2021027736
LC ebook record available at https://lccn.loc.gov/2021027737

Dedication

I dedicate this book to my parents, Bill and Louise Dodd, who loved boating and exposed me to the wonderful joys of the Chesapeake Bay.

Table of Contents

Dedication v

Introduction...1

Baltimore, Maryland...5

Annapolis, Maryland..16

Solomons Island, Maryland...24

Tall Timbers, Maryland on Herring Creek...........................30

Cobb Island, Maryland...33

Washington, D.C..40

Colonial Beach, Virginia...48

Reedville, Virginia..50

Irvington, Virginia..53

Yorktown, Virginia...57

Hampton, Virginia..61

Cape Charles, Virginia..67

Onancock, Virginia...71

Crisfield, Maryland...74

Cambridge, Maryland...82

Oxford, Maryland...86

St. Michaels, Maryland...89

Chestertown, Maryland...95

Rock Hall, Maryland...98

Fairlee Creek, Maryland..102

Georgetown (on the Sassafras River), Maryland 105

Chesapeake City and the C&D Canal (Back Creek), Maryland 109

Havre de Grace, Maryland...113

Summary and Conclusions...117

Appendix A-Additional Recommended Reading.....................120

Appendix B-Recipes 122

Acknowledgments...123

About the Author..124

"Time Out" docked at Ego Alley in Annapolis with the Maryland Statehouse in the background.

Introduction

This cruising guide is written for yachtsmen, sailors, powerboaters, and fishermen who may yearn to explore the beautiful Chesapeake Bay. The Bay is a vast and unique body of water. It has numerous rivers, creeks, canals, shallows, islands, and gunkholes. Its shores are home to important cities along with numerous charming towns and villages. To appreciate its beauty and enjoy its venues, we invite you to explore the Bay and enjoy the amazing history of this region. Included in the description of each port on our journey is a summary of interesting historical facts. In addition, many ports have unique features as one enters via water and brief descriptions of the entrance are offered when appropriate. Suggestions are made for marinas, restaurants, and local points of interest.

For boaters new to the Bay, we hope this guide entices you to explore this magnificent body of water.

For those acquainted with this region, we hope this guide whets your appetite to cruise into new, previously unexplored locations.

Enjoy.

Estuaries are bodies of water where salt water and fresh water intermingle. The Chesapeake Bay is the largest estuary in the United States. The major contributor of fresh water to the bay is the Susquehanna River. The Susquehanna is a giant funnel that drains lakes and streams from Pennsylvania, New York, and Maryland. Its northernmost origin is in Otsego Lake, New York. The river is 444 miles in length and is the nation's 16th largest. The water from this huge river is deposited into the northwestern part of the Bay at the city of Havre de Grace, Maryland.

A second major contributor of fresh water to the Chesapeake Bay is the Potomac River, the 21st largest river in the nation. It is 405 miles long. It collects fresh water from Pennsylvania, Maryland, Virginia, West Virginia, and the District of Columbia. There are other smaller rivers that contribute to the Bay. They include, from north to south, the Patapsco, Severn, Patuxent, Rappahannock, York, and James Rivers. All these rivers are on the "Western Shore" of the Chesapeake Bay and our journey will make stops at sites along each of them.

The "Eastern Shore" of the Bay has fewer rivers and they are smaller. Since the land mass of the Eastern Shore is quite flat, these rivers originate in swampy tidal areas. The Eastern Shore comprises the Delmarva Peninsula (DELaware, MARyland, VA for Virginia) and is serene and beautiful in the extreme. Our journey will include visits to the Choptank, Miles, Chester, Sassafras, Back Creek (C&D Canal), and several other small creeks.

The saltwater component of the Bay has its source at the southern end where the Bay meets the Atlantic Ocean. As one sails north the water loses its salty mix and north of Baltimore the water is brackish. The salt content has an impact on the fish, crabs, and many types of microorganisms which inhabit the Bay waters.

The Chesapeake Bay measures about 200 miles from the mouth of the Susquehanna River at the northern extreme, to the mouth of the

Bay at the Atlantic Ocean in the south. There is a narrow, man-made canal at the northeastern portion of the Bay called the Chesapeake and Delaware Canal, or C&D Canal. This Canal is 14 miles long and is deep enough to accommodate large ships. The canal connects the Chesapeake Bay to the Delaware River and the Atlantic Ocean. So, the Bay has a wide opening in the south and a narrow opening at its northern extreme, both of which connect it to the world.

At the Bay's widest point in the south, a boater in the middle can see no land. It is approximately 30 miles in width. As the Bay narrows at the top, it is about three miles wide. The average Bay depth is shallow; only about 20 feet. Yet, deep north-south channels allow enormous commercial and naval ships to course the Bay to the major port of Baltimore and through the C&D Canal. The deepest spot in the Bay is at Bloody Point near the mouth of Eastern Bay about 14 nautical miles southeast of Annapolis. It is said that the depth here is 174 feet in a small trough.

Because of its many rivers, streams, tributaries, and small bays, the Chesapeake Bay has a lengthy coastline. It is estimated to exceed 11,000 miles. Within this beautiful estuary, there may be as many as 2,500 species of plants, fish, and animals living in and around the Bay.

The other great asset of this magnificent estuary is the rich history of its shores. Many significant events of early American history took place in and around the Bay. As we visit our chosen cities and sites we will review and explore some of this interesting historic background which helped develop our magnificent Republic. Before we begin our exploration, starting in the city of Baltimore, I would like to introduce myself, offer a brief biography and go over a few technical points.

I was born in the port city of Baltimore when it was a quiet southern town. The year was 1946. My father, Bill Dodd, introduced me to boating at a young age. He loved the water, and he would take our family out for week-long trips on a 38-ft Chris Craft charter motorboat. He and my older brother would plot and chart a course, and operate the boat. If I was good, I was allowed to steer the vessel under direct supervision. We slept aboard nightly, under the silence of the clear Bay sky. This was before cell phones, even before TV, at least TV on a boat. Reading was encouraged.

I recall one other boating experience as a youngster. My father took us on an overnight cruise from Norfolk to Baltimore on a steamship of the Old Bay Line. Onboard was a dining room, a small dance floor, and comfortable staterooms for the overnight cruise up the Chesapeake Bay. Dad drove our car aboard. I am guessing the year was 1956. This Line may have been the last passenger steamship service in the US when it shut down in 1962.

Somehow those memories were planted in my brain and never deserted me. When I completed my training as an ophthalmologist, I got back into boating part-time. During that period, I learned to sail and spent consecutive summers on week-long overnight trips with my wife, Maureen. Later, we enjoyed chartering power boats with other couples and our children.

The memories grew.

Over time, I had accumulated many hours at the helm of various sail and power vessels and decided to test for a US Coast Guard Captain's License. I took an on-line didactic course for four months and then a qualifying exam, which I succeeded in passing. After a physical exam and laboratory tests, I was awarded a 50-Ton Inland Waterway License with a Masters addition. This allowed me to operate a vessel up to 50 tons for commercial purposes. At the time I had a motor yacht which I offered for charter. Because I still was working full time, I was unable to take out charters myself, so another captain was hired for that purpose. I have maintained my USCG Captain's license.

I now own a 1984 classic 61-ft Hatteras Cockpit Motor Yacht, which was designed by Jack Hargrave and constructed at the Hatteras plant in New Bern, North Carolina. Maureen and I are able to handle the vessel ourselves and there is room for up to four overnight guests to join us on our excursions. It is this vessel, named, *Time Out*, that we used to explore the Bay.

We both are retired, so we are not in a great hurry. We typically cruise at 9-10 knots (nautical miles per hour — see discussion below). This is a comfortable cruising speed and is not so hard on fuel consumption. It also makes distance/time calculations easy. If we have a goal of traveling 50 nautical miles, it will take us 5 hours at 10 knots. Simple is good.

When planning this trip, we decided to start in the historic and illustrious port of Baltimore, Maryland, and travel south to end the first leg in Hampton, Virginia. We wanted to follow a long loop, so we remained on the Western Shore as we went south. Included in this part of the trip, we cruised west and north up the Potomac River to visit Washington, D.C.

After terminating our first leg of the journey in Hampton, Virginia we crossed the Bay and cruised up the Eastern Shore of the Delmarva Peninsula.

One nice thing about the Bay is that it is relatively narrow and crossing back and forth from east to west is no problem for boaters and may be necessary depending on time constraints and weather conditions. We recognize that many boaters will not be able to replicate our exact journey at one time, but we wanted to lay it out for anyone interested and to highlight some of the many interesting places to visit by water. By no means have we exhausted all the potential spots to visit on the Bay. We may add more sites to this odyssey in the future.

This journey can be done in about 35 days. For those without much time, the journey can be broken into segments, of course. For those with more time, one can spend overnights indefinitely. Great ports in which to spend more time include Baltimore, Annapolis, Washington, D.C., Solomons Island, Hampton, and St. Michaels. And for those who prefer to anchor out, there are seemingly infinite numbers of gunkholes for that alternative.

The general format for the visit to each port is: HISTORY, ARRIVAL BY WATER, OVERNIGHT, SIGHTS, and EATERIES. Also, in capital letters, there are places of particular interest labeled POINT OF INTEREST.

I am not a historian by training, but I enjoy American History and I have spent my entire life around the Bay. I have read many fine works on Bay history, and I have included a bibliography in Appendix A for those who choose to dig deeper. In Appendix B, I have added a few topics which may be of interest to those who may not be acquainted with life on the Chesapeake Bay. For example, there is a recipe for steaming hard crabs which I have found is hard to beat.

To boaters new to the Bay, one must be made aware of "crab pots." These are 2.5-foot cubes made of a chicken-wire type grid and are used to catch the Bay's famous Blue Crabs. There are four round openings on the sides which allow the crabs to crawl into the trap but prohibit their exit. The crabs are attracted by the presence of bait which is placed in a cylinder on the top of the crab pot. The bait may be dead fish or chicken necks. Watermen may own dozens of these crab pots which they drop from the side of their work boats. Each crab pot has a colored float attached, sometimes with a small flag on top. Each waterman has his own distinct color to identify his property. The danger for all boaters occurs if one accidentally motors or sails over a crab pot and entangles the float and rope in their running gear. Should this happen, significant damage can be done to the prop, shaft, rudder, or hull. Typically, the waterman will place the crab pots in relatively shallow areas of 6 to 15 feet of depth. So, in these shallow areas, careful attention must be paid to avoid driving over a float. Incidentally, these floats are difficult to see at night.

In busy areas, there are channels designated by the state where crab pots may not be placed.

However, these "crab pot free zones" are not 100% reliable. Storms or high winds may push crab pots into these zones. The rule is "Keep Watch."

It is never appropriate or legal to disturb the crab pots or remove crabs from them. Watermen derive their livelihood from the Bay, and we all enjoy this bounty.

Should your prop get entangled in a crab pot line, stop the engine, drop anchor and if possible, get into the water to inspect. With luck you may be able to unwind the rope, if not you may need to cut it. If your prop is damaged, you will need to be towed in.

Many motor yachts have steel "cutters" on the prop shaft which will cut the rope as it begins to wrap around the shaft. The best advice is to watch carefully for the floats and avoid them.

Another interesting sight common on the Bay are the beautiful birds known as ospreys or sea hawks. They are fish-eating and often can be seen diving into the Bay waters and flying off with a nice meal. They build sturdy nests with sticks and frequently place their nests on the top of channel daymarks throughout the Bay. Ospreys seem to ignore the boat traffic which cruises close by the daymarks. In the spring they can be seen feeding their young. It is unlawful to disturb the birds or their nests.

Finally, regarding the use of the terms miles and nautical miles. Statute miles derive from the old English system utilizing feet and yards. One statute mile equals 5,280 feet (or 1,760 yards). In English-speaking countries, this is in standard usage for measuring distance on land. It turns out that since the circumference of the earth is accurately known, a nautical mile is a better way of dividing the earth's latitude. The technical definition of a nautical mile is: one minute of one degree of latitude. There are 60 minutes of latitude per degree. A nautical mile equals 6,080 feet; slightly more than a statute mile (one nautical mile converts to 1.15 statute miles). Sea captains and airplane pilots use nautical miles. One nautical mile per hour equals one knot of speed. So, if a boat is traveling at 9 knots (9 nautical miles per hour) that is equal to 10.35 statute miles per hour (9 knots x 1.15=10.35 mph). When we discuss speed on the water we will use "knots" and distances on the water in "nautical miles."

There are many charts available for cruising the Chesapeake Bay. My personal favorite is produced by Williams & Heintz Map Corporation. They print the "Maryland Cruising Guide" and the "Virginia Cruising Guide." These are in booklet form for easy use and measure 10.5"x15.25." Each page is water-resistant and contains accurate charting data, buoys, daymarks, water depth, suggested courses, and tidal information. They also include valuable information about every marina on the Bay. You can order their charts directly via their web address: **www.whmap.com**.

One final point must be mentioned. We made most of our trip during the summer of 2020. This was in the midst of the Covid 19 epidemic which struck our country. We abided by the rules for Maryland and Virginia at the time; that is, social distancing, wearing masks indoors, and frequent hand washing. Some of the places we visited had venues that were closed at the time. For example, the National Park Service at Yorktown was closed. But all marinas and fuel docks were open and functioning. These restrictions did not detract from the enjoyment and excitement of our trip and hopefully, in the near future, everything will be open and get back to normal.

I hope this manual will help you enjoy the beautiful and historic Chesapeake Bay. Happy Boating! And have fun!

NOTE: Directions on the water are intended to be accurate based on available charts as of 2019-2020 but cannot be guaranteed. Mariners must access all situations and note that some buoys and daymarks may move or be completely absent and suggested courses may vary.

Chapter 1
Baltimore, Maryland

HISTORY: The Port That Built a City

The Maryland General Assembly in 1706 authorized the Port of Baltimore at the northern tip of the Patapsco River where Jones Falls deposits fresh water from Baltimore County. The city is named for the Irish barony of Baltimore, seat of the Calvert family, proprietors of the Colony of Maryland. The city quickly prospered and with its deep water became known for its shipbuilding.

Baltimore obelisk

During the American Revolution, Baltimore saw no military action, but the Second Continental Congress held sessions there from December 1776 through February 1777.

Baltimore was intimately involved in the War of 1812. This war had multiple causes. Since the British were in a desperate struggle with France under Napoleon, the British wanted trade between the United States and France to cease. The British navy had been removing American seaman from neutral US commercial ships while at sea (impressment). In addition, the British and Canadians had concerns that the US had an expansionist policy toward Canada. It was the United States that declared war on the British in spite of the fact that the British had a far superior navy. Important battles during the War of 1812 took place on Lake Erie, the Chesapeake Bay, and in New Orleans.

The story of the path to the Star-Spangled Banner song is somewhat convoluted but begins here on the Chesapeake Bay in 1813. For years, the British had been bothered by privateers from Baltimore who interfered with their shipping trade. When the War of 1812 commenced, the British Crown gave the responsibility of punishing Bay inhabitants to

Vice-Admiral Sir Alex Cochrane. Cochrane then gave the dirty work to Rear Admiral George Cockburn, who seemed to enjoy the grizzly task. The years of 1813-1814 were difficult for the residents of Maryland, Virginia, and the District of Columbia. During the spring of 1813, Cockburn pressed his advantage utilizing the considerable fleet and the well-trained men at his disposal. He blockaded the Chesapeake Bay, attacking and burning many towns. At the mouth of the Susquehanna River he burned the town of Havre de Grace in May 1813. He repeated this action on the Sassafras River burning the towns of Fredericktown and Georgetown. He gallivanted about the northern Bay without interference. He destroyed the munitions plant and the famous Iron Works at Principio Furnace (just northeast of Havre de Grace) where American cannons were made.

The British then decided to attack and burn the nascent Capital in Washington, D.C. in response to the American attack on York, Canada in April 1813. The most obvious sea route to Washington was up the Chesapeake Bay to the Potomac River. However, the Potomac was difficult because of many shallows and shoals. But the Potomac was poorly defended, and a small British Naval force successfully attacked Alexandria, Virginia, and looted that prosperous community (more details under our visit to Washington, D.C.). Meanwhile, the main British attacking force, under Admiral George Cockburn, was sent up the adjacent Patuxent River. Here, the British encountered some opposition by a group of about 18 American long boats and gun barges (measuring only 50 to 75 feet) under Commodore Joshua Barney. His small flotilla was involved in the largest naval engagement in Maryland history. The first battles with the British frigates occurred on June 8-10, 1814, at St Leonard Creek, an eastern tributary of the Patuxent River. After an exchange of gunfire over two days, the larger British fleet totaling 45 vessels, trapped Barney in the narrow creek. Since their larger deep-draft vessels could not pursue Barney into the creek, British marines

disembarked and instigated a reign of terror by raiding farms and towns in the vicinity. The Courthouse in Prince Frederick, the county seat of Calvert County, was burned. Similar attacks by the British were carried out on the western side of the Patuxent into St. Mary's County. On June 26, 1814, with assistance on land from gathering American marines and militia, the second phase of the Battle of St. Leonard Creek developed. During intense firing on the British ships by the militia from land and from Commodore Barney at sea, his flotilla was able to escape from St. Leonard Creek and sail north to the narrows of the Patuxent. As the British sailed their frigates up the Patuxent River in pursuit, they shelled and bombarded any American farmhouses visible from the River.

The British fleet continued north to disembark troops on August 19, 1814, under General Robert Ross, at the tiny hamlet of Benedict, Maryland. General Ross had extensive experience fighting in Europe in the Napoleonic Wars. Ironically, James Monroe, then the Secretary of State and future President, served as a scout and reported to President James Madison in Washington, D.C. on the number of British ships collecting at Benedict. From Benedict, the British army troops marched through Upper Marlboro to Bladensburg, Maryland on the eastern edge of the Capital. There, a significant battle took place on August 24th, with many of Commodore Barney's marines participating. The British sustained losses but pushed the Americans aside, leaving the way open to Washington. At this point, President James Madison and most government officials evacuated the Capital. Dolly Madison is remembered for rescuing from the White House as many historic artifacts as she could fit in the wagons, including the famous Gilbert Stuart portrait of George Washington.

On the evening of August 24, 1814, the British burned most government buildings in the new Capital including the White House, the Capital Building, and the Library of Congress.

A severe storm blew through Washington, D.C. late that night and heavy rains helped extinguish the fires.

As the British returned to their ships at Benedict, they passed back through the town of Upper Marlboro. They arrested an American physician, Dr. William Beanes. There were some accusations that he had not given proper care to British troops who were injured, and he had locked up British stragglers who were allegedly looting. After his capture, he was ensconced on a prison ship, the *HMS Tonnant*. The entire British fleet then set sail out of the Patuxent River into the Bay, to recommission at Tangier Island. The next site of an attack was the port of Baltimore where, because of Dr. William Beanes, history was about to be made.

Baltimore was infamous for its privateers that pestered the British commercial vessels. It was now time for paybacks. The British Navy, still under Admiral George Cockburn, developed a two-pronged attack for the port of Baltimore. The first part was a landing of 5,000 army troops under General Ross at North Point on the eastern shore of the Patapsco. They planned to march north for 12 miles to attack the City of Baltimore. In the second part, the fleet would approach by sea and attack and destroy Fort McHenry which blocked access to the city. Once past the Fort, the British Navy could directly bombard the city. Baltimore had warnings of the British arrival after their successful attack on Washington, D.C., and the residents took time to develop defensive fortifications so they would not suffer the same fate as the nation's Capital. The militia was formed and a vigorous defense was planned.

The land Battle of North Point did not go well for the British. During the battle, near the headwaters of Bear Creek, General Robert Ross was shot and killed by two teenage members of the militia, Henry McComas and Daniel Wells. Subsequently, they were killed by British troops. The date was September 12, 1814.

To this day, a monument, consisting of a 20-foot obelisk, stands at the corner of Monument Street and Asquith Street to honor the memory of McComas and Wells for their contribution to the defense of the city of Baltimore.

In addition to the loss of General Ross, the bombardment of Fort McHenry did not go as planned.

Francis Scott Key was a prominent attorney who worked in Frederick and Georgetown. He learned of Dr. Beanes' capture and went, with permission of President Madison, via sloop, to the *HMS Tonnant* to negotiate the release of Dr. Beanes. The *HMS Tonnant* was anchored with the British Fleet in the Chesapeake Bay near Tangier Island. Key was able to convince the British to release Beanes with written statements of British officers who had been treated well by Beanes in Upper Marlboro. Although Key succeeded in freeing Dr. Beanes, Key was held aboard the ship for several nights because he had overheard the British plan of attack on Baltimore. Once the British ships, numbering over 45 vessels, sailed up the Chesapeake Bay into the Patapsco River and anchored in Baltimore harbor, the brutal overnight bombardment of Fort McHenry began. Intermittently, over 24 hours, the British bombarded the Fort with some 1,500 cannonballs, shells, and rockets. Early on the morning of September 14, 1814, from the deck of the British ship, Key observed that the American flag still flew over the Fort. Key began scribbling words for a song about the sights he had seen. This became known as the Star-Spangled Banner. Those words were officially designated as our National Anthem in 1931 when President Herbert Hoover signed a Congressional Resolution.

In the meantime, on land, the denizens of Baltimore created a 3-mile trench from the Canton district of the city northeast to Belair Road to block the British land invasion as the army continued their march from North Point. In spite of the loss of General Ross, the British planned to attack the city on September 13,

1814. But as the army approached and observed the impressive fortifications, they realized this was not going to be as easy as their attack on Washington. The army wisely retired and returned to their ships.

After surprising American resistance, significant troop losses, the death of General Ross, and failure to destroy Fort McHenry, the British weighed anchor and departed on September 14, 1814, never to return. Baltimore was saved. The next destination of the British navy was New Orleans where they suffered a devastating loss at the hands of General Andrew Jackson.

Fort McHenry was named after a Revolutionary War veteran Dr. James McHenry. He served as an aid to Washington during the War. Later, he was appointed as a delegate to the Constitutional Convention in Philadelphia. McHenry was one of three signers of the United States Constitution from the state of Maryland. He later served in the Maryland House of Delegates and subsequently in the Maryland Senate. Under the Washington administration, he was appointed as the first Secretary of War. McHenry is credited with establishing the US Department of the Navy.

Fort McHenry lived on to make additional historic contributions to our nation. During the Civil War, Maryland was a border state whose citizens were split with sympathies for both the North and South. Since Washington, D.C. is surrounded on the east and north by Maryland, President Lincoln could ill afford to have Maryland secede from the Union. In the State Legislature, there was an effort to pass an Act of Secession. Lincoln sent Federal Union troops into Baltimore to maintain order, and it was there that the first casualties of the Civil War occurred. In addition, the Union troops were ordered to arrest certain members of the State Legislature. Those who were apprehended were jailed at Fort McHenry until the end of the hostilities. Additional citizens interred at Fort McHenry included the Mayor of Baltimore, the city council, the police commissioner, several newspaper editors and owners, and ironically, Francis Key Howard, the grandson of Francis Scott Key. Incidentally, Lincoln violated the US Constitution by arresting these men who had not committed a crime (Article I, Section 9, paragraph 2, the Writ of Habeas Corpus. This can be suspended during an insurrection only by Congress, not the President).

In addition, during the Civil War, Confederate POWs were housed at Fort McHenry.

There is one more fort of some interest in the Patapsco River south of the port of Baltimore. It is Fort Carroll, a small island on the east side of the River just south of the Key Bridge (named after Francis Scott Key, of course). Fort Carroll was built in 1852 to create another layer of protection for Baltimore from attack by sea. The Fort was built by Robert E. Lee of the US Army Corps of Engineers. Although it is now abandoned, the Fort still is visible today as a flat, shrub-covered island surrounded by a bulkhead of old pilings and populated with squawking birds.

Finally, during World War I, in 1917, Fort McHenry was converted into a temporary 3,000-bed hospital. After that war, in 1925, the Fort was established as a National Park.

There is another area of interest regarding Baltimore's history. The first passenger railroad in the United States was established here. The Baltimore and Ohio (B&O) was created in 1829 to carry passengers and freight to the far west, i.e. Ohio. The railroad was built to compete with river traffic going west through the recently completed Erie Canal. Today, there is a wonderful train museum at 901 West Pratt Street, the B&O Railroad Museum. This is the Mt. Clare Station, the oldest railroad manufacturing complex in the United States. It was designated as a National Historic Landmark in 1961.

Baltimore has a reputation as having an excellent medical community. Many Maryland physicians have trained at one of the two outstanding medical schools in downtown Baltimore. The University of Maryland School of Medicine was established in 1807, making it the fifth oldest medical school in the nation and the first public medical school. Later, the Johns Hopkins School of Medicine was created in 1893 utilizing the donated fortune of the well-to-do Quaker merchant, Johns Hopkins, and donations of wealthy daughters of prominent local businessmen. Their donations were contingent on allowing women to be admitted to study medicine.

Depending on the season of your visit, you should check out the team schedules to see if they are playing in town.

One final bit of local history. Glenn L. Martin was an early pioneer pilot who opened an aircraft manufacturing facility in 1929 outside of Baltimore at the headwaters of the Middle River. Martin's firm built three of the famous "China Clipper" sea planes or "flying boats," that flew from San Francisco to Manila and had comfortable sleeping berths. The 60-hour trip was spread out over five days with

Photo used with permission from "Martin Seamaster P6M, Piet and Raithel

Glenn L. Martin SeaMaster flying jet boat

The world's first dental school, the Baltimore College of Dental Surgery, was established in Baltimore in 1840 and is now part of the University of Maryland system.

Finally, Baltimore is home to professional sports. There are two stadiums near the Inner Harbor. The first is Oriole Park at Camden Yards, where the Baltimore Orioles professional baseball team plays. Incidentally, Babe Ruth was born in Baltimore and the Babe Ruth Museum is located at 216 Emory Street. For baseball fans, it is worth a visit.

The second is the M&T (Bank) Stadium where the Baltimore Ravens professional football team plays. Both stadiums are a short Uber ride away from the Inner Harbor marinas.

a stopover in Honolulu, Midway, Wake, and Guam. The residents along Middle River recall seeing these four-engine behemoths practicing take-offs and landings.

During World War II, the Martin Company designed and built many types of airplanes for the military, including a variety of sea planes. The largest of these sea planes was the "Martin Mars" which was 120 feet long with a wingspan of 200 feet. When the War ended, so did the demand for "flying boats." But Glenn Martin did not lose interest and in the 1950s his company developed the first flying jet boat with four powerful engines. The flying jet boat was known as the P6M SeaMaster.

The Navy was interested in an intercontinental jet bomber that could carry nuclear

Baltimore Inner Harbor

weapons across the ocean and be refueled on the water by submarines. However, the SeaMaster flying jet boat did not have a long lifespan. In December 1955, one of the SeaMasters broke up in flight and crashed into the water at Point Lookout near the mouth of the Potomac River. A year later a second plane crashed over Odessa, DE. Then the Navy lost interest when newer jets could make round trip flights halfway around the world without stopping to refuel.

When I was a youngster on the Chris Craft charter boat with my family, we watched with fascination one of the P6M SeaMaster flying jet boats take off from the Middle River outside of Baltimore. It sprinted out toward the Bay for what seemed like forever before struggling into the air. The most memorable thing I recall was the formidable spray created around the plane and the near unbearable noise.

The **Glenn L. Martin Maryland Aviation Museum** (410-682-6122) is located at the Martin Airport southeast of Baltimore. It is worth a visit.

ARRIVAL BY WATER

Deep-draft ships heading to and from Baltimore will compete with any small craft entering the Patapsco River. The central Brewerton Channel is the main shipping channel for ships and is well-marked starting just beyond the mouth of the river. Coming from the south, I recommend picking up Green "3" on the south side of the Channel and cruise into the Harbor staying on the south side of the Channel through the Key Bridge up to Green "FM" just short of Fort McHenry.

As you pick up Green "3" look due north for a peninsula of land: that is North Point where the British disembarked for their invasion of Baltimore on September 12, 1814.

POINT OF INTEREST

When passing Green "11" if you gaze to starboard, you will see the vague remnants of the huge Sparrows Point steel mill; now largely disassembled. As you approach the Key Bridge (vert. clear 185') on the starboard side, you will see a flat island overgrown with shrubs: this is the remnant of Robert E. Lee's Fort Carroll. To the right of the old fort is the mouth of Bear Creek. General Robert Ross was killed near the headwaters of this creek. A low bridge prohibits exploration of the headwaters of Bear Creek.

Fort McHenry is straight ahead as you proceed under the Key Bridge. About halfway between the Key Bridge and Fort McHenry is where the British fleet was anchored for their bombardment. They stayed just beyond the reach of the Fort's many guns.

As you cruise toward the Fort, if you look to port and starboard you will see multiple cranes and docks in the busy port. Tugboats may be busy directing commercial ships. Baltimore is a large port for delivery of automobiles from foreign countries. The ships that carry them are distinct and odd-looking; the shape of a shoe box floating on the surface.

After arriving at the Green "FM" buoy, stay to starboard to enter the main waterway to downtown Baltimore. This waterway is known as the Inner Harbor. To port you will pass Fort McHenry; check it out with binoculars. You are now in a NO WAKE zone, so slow to five knots. To port and starboard you will see Navy ships, then multiple large marinas to starboard. Continue up the center of the channel. Many new tall buildings will present themselves as you approach the center of the City. To port, you will see a large dock at the Domino Sugar Plant. If you are fortunate you may see the huge scoops lifting sugar out of the hull of a ship docked at the Plant. The smell of unrefined sugar will fill your nostrils.

OVERNIGHT

There are many fine marinas to tie up and overnight on your vessel while in Baltimore. On the south side of the inner harbor, I have docked overnight at the Harborview Marina and Yacht Club.

- **Harborview Marina and Yacht Club–** They have 278 newly refurbished floating piers that can accommodate vessels up to 300 feet. Amenities include secure gated access, cable television, Wi-Fi, parking, outdoor pool, health club, bath facilities, laundry, and a boater's lounge. Several restaurants are on-site.

The marina is within walking distance of the many Baltimore attractions, festivities, restaurants, and the Orioles and Ravens stadiums.

Waypoint: 39° 16' N / 76° 36.1 W
Phone: 410-752-1122
Email: info@harborviewmarinecenter.com

On the north side of the Inner Harbor, I often dock at the Harbor East Marina.

• **Harbor East Marina**–They have 185 slips with floating docks, free pump-out, Wi-Fi, and other amenities. There is a Whole Foods store within walking distance, and Four Seasons and Marriott Hotels within two blocks, along with many restaurants and shops. For visitors, the marina offers a very nice free booklet that has a useful map and lists of local attractions.
Waypoint: 39° 16.883' N / 76° 36.083' W
Phone: 410-625-1700
Email: harboreastmarina@harboreast.com

• **Baltimore Marine Center at Inner Harbor** is another large marina closer to downtown and two blocks from the Maryland Science Center. The marina has 135 slips and offers gas and diesel fuel. On-site, The Rusty Scupper restaurant is easy to see to port as you approach.
Waypoint: 39.2773° N / 76.5789° W
Phone: 410-837-5339
Email:
    innerharbormarina@oasismarinas.com

SIGHTS

Within walking distance of the Harbor East Marina, I would recommend the following:

• **The National Aquarium**–Great for adults and children. If youngsters are aboard, you should also check out the Port Discovery Children's Museum that is nearby.
Phone: 410-576-3800
501 E. Pratt Street

• **The Maryland Science Center**–Another place for young and old. It has a wonderful planetarium, science exhibits, gift shop, and an IMAX theatre.
Phone: 410-685-5225
601 Light Street

• **Pier Six Pavilion**–Concerts and other events occur here. Depending on wind direction you sometimes can hear the concerts from your boat.

• **Water Taxi**–Enjoy a trip on the Water Taxi. Check **baltimorewatertaxi.com** for schedules, pick-up docks, and ticket costs.
Phone: 410-563-3900

• **Historic Ships and a Classic Screw-Pile Lighthouse**–Check out **historicships.org** to obtain tickets to visit four historic ships docked in Baltimore Harbor and a classic lighthouse.
Phone: 410-396-3453
1417 Thames Street

  a. **USS Torsk** is a WW II submarine that sank the last Japanese ship of the war on August 14, 1945. It was later used as a training vessel and recorded the most dives of any submarine.

  b. **USS Constellation**–The *USS Constellation* was built in 1855. This three-masted warship is the one remaining US Navy sloop-of-war.

  c. **USCG Taney** is a Coast Guard rescue and patrol ship that is the last remaining ship afloat that fought against the Japanese during their attack on Pearl Harbor on December 7, 1941. (In October 2020, this vessel was towed into a dry dock for repairs).

  d. **Chesapeake Lightship** served as a floating, movable lighthouse at the mouth of the Bay.

  e. **Seven Foot Knoll Lighthouse** This screw-pile lighthouse was constructed in 1856 at the mouth of the Patapsco River.

All these sights are open to the public, and each is worth seeing.

USS Constellation docked at Baltimore's Inner Harbor

- **<u>The Baltimore Museum of Industry</u>**–This quiet, less well-known museum is worth a half-day visit. It has on display the enormous varieties of inventions and innovations that helped make Baltimore an industrial powerhouse.
Phone: 410-727-4808
1415 Key Highway

- **<u>Take a walk</u>** around the community of Harbor East. There also are many shops and restaurants that are nearby Harbor Place and the Gallery (where the *USS Constellation* is docked).

- **Babe Ruth Museum** provides entertaining, cultural, and educational experiences through dynamic exhibits and programs at the birthplace of Babe Ruth. Check out baberuthmuseum.org for details.
Phone: 410-727-1539
216 Emory Street

- **Have Happy Hour** on the deck of your vessel and enjoy the sounds and sights of this active and lovely waterfront community. Invite your boating neighbor to join you.

Other must-see attractions beyond walking distance include:

- **Fort McHenry**–As noted in the HISTORY section, much of Baltimore's culture and lore revolves around this remarkable site. There is a museum with many artifacts and a short movie. The fort itself can be explored on foot, cannons can be inspected, and ramparts viewed. One can look down the Patapsco and imagine the incoming British bombs dropping from the sky. Allow about two hours.

- **B&O Railroad Museum**–This historic museum, located in an enormous round house, contains dozens of old train engines and passenger cars. There is a gift shop and the museum is child-friendly. A short train ride is available. Check **borail.org** for details. Allow 3-4 hours. Do not miss this.
Phone: 410-752-2490
901 W Pratt Street

- **Fells Point**–This charming neighborhood on the water is a short drive or a long walk from the Harbor East Marina. There are many shops and eateries. It is easy to spend half a day checking out this fun area.

- **Glenn L. Martin Maryland Aviation Museum**–The museum is open on Wednesdays and Saturdays from 11:00 a.m.

to 3:00 p.m. and by appointment for private tours on other days. Worth a 25-minute drive from the Inner Harbor via Uber.
Phone: 410-682-6122
701 Wilson Pt. Road

- **Little Italy**–Known for its clean neighborhoods and wonderful Italian restaurants, it is worth an Uber ride for dinner.

If possible, spend a minimum of three days to see the significant sights in Baltimore.

EATERIES

There are too many excellent restaurants in Baltimore to list them all. We will list here a few of our favorites in the Inner Harbor area.

- **Charleston** offers an extensive prix fixe tasting menu from which you can choose from among six courses. The wait service is experienced, informed, and very intuitive.
Phone: 410-332-7373
1000 Lancaster Street

- **Nicks Fish House** serves seafood, regional specialties, and steamed crabs. The menu has something for everyone from deck fries to their famous crab cakes.
Phone: 410-347-4123
2600 Insular Drive

- **Azumi** offers an interactive dining experience featuring menu items prepared right before your eyes in a relaxed setting. The cooking technique of Azumi's highly-skilled chefs is on full display in their Flame Room as they prepare your selections on a solid-surface iron griddle right in front of you.
Phone: 443-220-0477
725 Aliceanna Street

- **The Oceanaire Seafood Room** strives to provide you with the freshest seafood experience. The menu features both seasonal and sustainable seafood that is flown in fresh daily.
Phone: 443-872-0000
801 Aliceanna Street

- **Bar Vasquez** brings the vibrancy and energy of Buenos Aires to Baltimore's harbor and reflects the Argentine love of meat, fire, and seasonal ingredients. Friday and Saturday evenings, live music is performed by local musicians.
Phone: 410-534-7296
1425 Aliceanna Street

- **Bygone** at the top of the Four Seasons Hotel. They offer a seasonally driven menu, showcasing ingredients at their peak in season. The rotisserie oven is the fulcrum of the kitchen. Whole birds, wild game, meat and fish are slow-roasted over an open fire and presented table-side. They believe in sourcing from the region whenever possible and consistently building relationships with local farmers, fishermen, and foragers.
Phone: 443-343-8200
400 International Drive

- **Tio Pepe** serves authentic, homemade Spanish and Mediterranean food. They start with the freshest ingredients and use authentic recipes to create an array of meals that are sure to satisfy.
Phone: 410-539-4675
10 E Franklin Street
You will need an Uber.

NEXT DESTINATION: ANNAPOLIS, MARYLAND - 26 Miles

We always attempt to depart from our destinations at sunrise. This way you get the travel part accomplished early and you can spend the remainder of the day at your new port. Sunrise is also the best time to take photos. While underway you can plan your day at the next stop.

The trip from Baltimore to Annapolis is only 26 miles, so this short journey could allow an opportunity to sleep in and cast off a bit later. For those who would like to put in a longer trip at sea, you could bypass Annapolis, but visit later on the northern leg of the trip. In no case should Annapolis be deleted from your itinerary. It is the crown jewel of the Chesapeake Bay and full of interesting history and sights, as we soon will see. The next stop south, if you bypass Annapolis, is Solomon's Island that is 68 miles from Baltimore. But here we will assume our destination is historic Annapolis, the beautiful Capital city of Maryland.

Chapter 2
Annapolis, Maryland
HISTORY

Entire books are available with details about the long and fascinating history of Annapolis. What is presented here is a brief outline. Check Appendix A for additional reading suggestions.

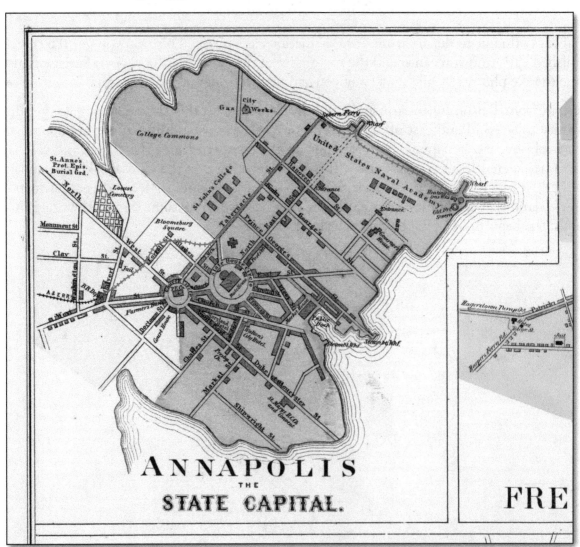

From *Lincoln in Annapolis, February 1865,* with permission, Maryland State Archives"

The dotted red line tracks Abraham Lincoln's walking path through Annapolis to the Naval Academy pier to board the Thomas Collyer steamship on February 2, 1865.

Historic Middleton Tavern at the foot of Ego Alley

English Puritans migrated from Virginia to establish a settlement at the site of present-day Annapolis around 1649. The early history of Maryland was reflected in the religious controversies between Protestants and Catholics erupting in England during this era. One of the early names for Annapolis was 'Providence,' but was later changed to 'Anne Arundel's Town.' Lady Anne Arundel was the wife of Cecil Calvert, the second Lord Baltimore, who was the designated proprietor of Maryland. Anne Arundel County remains as her namesake with the city of Annapolis as its County Seat and the State Capital.

In 1694, Royal Governor Francis Nicholson renamed the town. He took the moniker of English Princess Anne, who later would become the Queen of England. He combined her name with the Greek word for city, "polis" as the suffix. In that same year, the Capital city of Maryland was transferred from St. Mary's City to Annapolis.

During the 18th Century, Annapolis grew and prospered. Farmers toiled the fertile land in Anne Arundel County and points south and shipped their produce and tobacco to the expanding port city. Imports included rum, furniture, and sadly, slaves. The author, Alex Haley, composed a compelling historic novel in 1976 (Roots) about his ancestor imported to the colonies via the port of Annapolis. Today, a bronze statue of a seated Alex Haley, with several children around him, is located in the center of Annapolis at the harbor.

Annapolis grew as a political and administrative center and was known as the "Athens of America." During this period merchants and landowners built remarkable homes that remain today as a tribute to the wealth and growth of the city. Culture and the arts flourished and the first theatre in America was built in Annapolis. In Colonial times Annapolis boasted a racetrack where, allegedly, George Washington complained of losing money.

As the American Revolution enveloped the colonies, Annapolis was peripherally involved. There were four signers of the Declaration of Independence from Maryland, and all were from Annapolis. They were wealthy and their luxurious homes remain essentially intact and are within walking distance of the Annapolis Harbor. The signers were: Charles Carroll of Carrollton, Samuel Chase, William Paca, and Thomas Stone.

Carroll's home is located behind St. Mary's Catholic Church and is available for tours. Carroll was probably the wealthiest man in the Colonies and the only Catholic signer. He lived the longest of any signer.

Samuel Chase was appointed to the Supreme Court of the United States in 1796 by George Washington. His large house is now a retirement home for women.

William Paca (rhymes with TAKE A) was an attorney and aside from signing the Declaration of Independence served as the Governor of Maryland and a US District Court Judge. In addition, he served in the Maryland Senate and the House of Delegates. His home is now a beautifully restored museum and is open to the public.

Thomas Stone was an attorney and wealthy planter who owned the Peggy Stewart House from 1783 to 1787. In 1772, the House was owned originally by Anthony Stewart who also was the owner of the merchant ship, "*Peggy Stewart*," which is discussed below. The home is now in private hands and not open to the public.

The burning and sinking of the merchant ship, "*Peggy Stewart*" in Annapolis was a miniature version of the Boston Tea Party. This incident involved the surreptitious importation of tea to avoid a tax. The citizens of Annapolis were agitated and they coerced the owners to burn the ship with the tea onboard on October 19, 1774.

Of interest is that the signers of the Declaration of Independence were not traditional radicals from the bottom of the social hierarchy, but rather men of education and considerable wealth; i.e. the aristocracy.

No Revolutionary War battles occurred in the vicinity of Annapolis, although a fort was built in Annapolis on the Severn River to protect the city from a potential British attack (Fort Severn). However, Marquis de La Fayette did encamp on the south side of Spa Creek during March and April of 1781. He was on his way to engage the British in Virginia. Washington later joined La Fayette in Virginia and together they participated in the siege of Yorktown that ended in victory for the Americans and was the last significant battle of the Revolutionary War.

We will discuss this engagement in more detail when we visit Yorktown, Virginia.

Likely, the most famous event that occurred in Annapolis was the voluntary resignation of General George Washington from his role as Commander of the Continental Army on December 23, 1783 at the Maryland State House. At that time, the State House was serving as the Capital of the States. Then, a month later, on January 14, 1784, the Treaty of Paris was ratified in the State House, officially ending the conflict with Great Britain. Two years later, in September of 1786, the Annapolis Convention of the States, meeting in the State House, issued the call to go to Philadelphia to modify the Articles of Confederation. What came out during the summer of 1787 in Philadelphia was more than a modification of the Articles, but rather an entirely new document, the Constitution of the United States.

During the War of 1812, Annapolis had no significant role and was not involved in any battles. Of interest, Francis Scott Key lived in Annapolis during his years as a student at St. John's College. As noted under the Baltimore History section, he was instrumental in releasing Dr. William Beanes from the British prison ship and Key composed the Star-Spangled Banner after observing the bombardment of Fort McHenry. During his years in Annapolis, Key resided in the Upton Scott House, a classic Georgian 18th Century home completed in 1765. It is now a private residence.

In 1845, the US Naval Academy was established under Secretary of the Navy, George Bancroft. The site chosen was the old Fort Severn at the mouth of Spa Creek where it joins the Severn River. The Academy's Bancroft Hall is the largest college dormitory in the world with accommodations for some 4,000 midshipmen during their four years of training at the Naval Academy. It is said to have over four miles of corridors.

With the outset of the Civil War on April 12, 1861, Annapolis again was peripherally involved although no battles occurred nearby. The State of Maryland was known for its Southern sympathies. The Legislature was considering an Act of Secession, thus putting Lincoln and the Unionists in a difficult spot. If Maryland seceded and joined the rebellious Southern States, Washington, D.C. would be surrounded by states in rebellion. On orders from the President, federal troops were sent into Maryland and the entire legislature was arrested and placed in jail (some at Fort McHenry) until members swore an oath of loyalty to the Union. As more Southern states began to secede from the Union, midshipmen at the Naval Academy who resided in the South, departed and went home. In May 1861, the Naval Academy moved its midshipmen and instructors to Newport, Rhode Island. During the Civil War, the buildings at the Naval Academy were used as a hospital until the War ended on April 9, 1865.

The other institution of higher learning in Annapolis is St. John's College, the third oldest in America (after Harvard and William and Mary). During the Civil War the college was converted to a military camp to house injured soldiers and exchange Union prisoners.

On February 2, 1865, Abraham Lincoln paid a brief visit to Annapolis just two months before his death (April 15, 1865). Lincoln secretly took a train from Washington, D.C. to Annapolis and disembarked at the station on the corner of West Street and Calvert Street. He walked about 1.5 miles to the wharf at the Naval Academy with only his bodyguard, his valet, and a quartermaster. They walked past the Maryland State House (where the Thirteenth Amendment to end slavery was being debated that very day), along College Avenue past St. John's College, where Union soldiers were bivouacked, and then onto the Naval Academy grounds. He boarded a fast steamer, the *Thomas Collyer*. His destination was Fort Monroe at Hampton, Virginia where he and his Secretary of State, William Seward met with three representatives of the Confederate States of America to negotiate the end of the Civil War. The negotiations did not go well because Lincoln would not agree to an independent South and

the Confederates would not agree to rejoin the Union. Lincoln departed that day to return to Annapolis and then back to Washington, D.C. empty-handed.

During the Civil War, there was another interesting visitor to Annapolis. Composer Rimsky-Korsakov was a sailor aboard the Russian Naval Clipper Ship *"Almaz"* The ship visited several east coast cities and spent the month of February 1864 anchored in the Severn River. The composer made many visits to the restaurants and taverns in Annapolis.

Another celebrity visited Annapolis. Elizabeth, the Queen Mother of England, visited Annapolis on November 8, 1954. She drove around town in an open convertible with Governor Theodore McKeldin. The reason for the visit was apparently social.

With this fascinating background about historic Annapolis, a mariner tied up at any local marina will likely need at least two days to appreciate this port. Fortunately, Annapolis is a walking town and small enough to take in the entire enterprise by foot.

ARRIVAL BY WATER

Coming south from Baltimore you will pass beneath the magnificent Chesapeake Bay Bridges, parallel spans that connect the Western and Eastern Shores of Maryland. The original south span of the Bay Bridge was completed in 1952. Prior to that year there were large ferry boats which traversed the bay with people, cargo, trucks, and cars. The remnants of a ferry boat dock can be seen on the western side of the Bridge. The Bay Bridge had a significant impact on the growth of the entire Eastern Shore including the beach communities of Ocean City, Maryland, and Rehoboth Beach, Delaware. The channel for deep-draft ships is the Craighill Channel. To the starboard side of Baltimore Light is the mouth of the lovely Magothy River. You will pass Gibson Island, a beautiful gated community surrounded by the Bay on the east and the Magothy River on the west. The Gibson Island Yacht Club is a small yacht club on the River side.

I generally cruise a course parallel to Craighill Channel and go under the western high spans of the bridges. Once under the bridges steer gently to starboard and honor Red Flashing "4" at Greenbury Point. This marks the mouth of the Severn River with Annapolis about a mile away. Two prominent domes are present over Annapolis; the Naval Academy to the right and the State House slightly to the left. To port, honor Horn Point, "HP Flashing." Legend says that a barge carrying George Washington ran aground in the shallows of the Horn Point shoals. As you enter Spa Creek, the large building to starboard is Bancroft Hall and the large athletic fields of the US Naval Academy.

OVERNIGHT

The most popular place to secure a slip is located in the center of town at the narrow 200-yard-long mini-harbor, known as Ego Alley. One can tie up here by securing a slip with the Harbormaster at the Annapolis City Dock. There are about 31 slips for public docking. All have water and electric. They rent by the hour, day, or week. These slips are popular because they are at the center of the action. Boats of all shapes and sizes putter in and out of Ego Alley during the day. Pedestrian walkways are full as tourists and locals enjoy the scenery, the water, and the boats. A small park at the end of the city dock is a gathering place and often has music, dancing, or shows. Check **www.annapolis.gov** for info on activities there and around the town. Market House is at the terminus of Ego Alley and offers food and refreshments. Also, at the end of Ego Alley is the bronze statue of a seated Alex Haley and several children. There are at least a half dozen restaurants within eyesight of the city dock.

Reservations at Annapolis City Dock are needed for overnight stays. For weekends there is a 2-night minimum. Call 3-4 weeks in advance to be sure you can obtain a slip. The dockmasters office is on the starboard side of Ego Alley. Male and female bathrooms and showers are located on the second floor. I have seen cleaner. If you overnight on weekends be warned that some of the bars do not close until 1:00 a.m. and it can get a bit noisy at that hour.

The dockmaster also controls the mooring balls in the mouth of Spa Creek. If you have a dingy and do not miss seeing all the action on Ego Alley, these mooring balls are a much less expensive alternative than tying up at the city dock. Even if you don't have a dinghy, there is a water taxi that will pick you up and drop you off at a variety of stops for a small fee. Call the Water Taxi on VHF channel 68.

There are two grand yacht clubs in Annapolis. If you belong to a yacht club at your home port, check out to see if they reciprocate.

- The world-famous **Annapolis Yacht Club** has a few overnight slips and several day slips for members and guests. Their food is excellent. Reservations are required. The club is on the starboard side of Spa Creek just short of the Draw Bridge.
  Phone: 410-263-9279
  2 Compromise Street

- The **Eastport Yacht Club** is on the port side as you turn into Spa Creek. They sometimes have a few slips available for overnight stays. They have an excellent restaurant and a bar that looks out over the Severn River.
  Phone: 410-267-9549
  317 First Street

Another fine marina located downtown is the Annapolis Yacht Basin.

- **Annapolis Yacht Basin** offers a large, modern facility with 100 fixed slips and three deep water face docks for vessels up to 240 feet. Amenities include electricity, pump-out, fuel, showers, laundry room, Wi-Fi, and cable TV.

  Overnighting here is quieter than at the Annapolis City Dock.
  Waypoint: 38° 58' 43" N / 76° 29' 13" W
  Phone: 410-263-3544
  2 Compromise Street

Maryland State House

• **Maryland State House**–At the top of the list of sights to see must be the Maryland State House. It sits majestically at the highest point in the city. It is the oldest state house in the nation in continuous use. The dome is wooden and was completed in 1797 and is the largest wooden dome in the United States constructed without nails. The House and Senate chambers are outlined in beautiful Italian marble. There are many historic paintings throughout the classic building.

As noted, the old Senate Chamber is where the Colonial Congress assembled on December 23, 1783 to accept the resignation of General George Washington from the Continental Army. The act symbolically established the concept of civilian authority over the military, that remains an important tradition in our country today.

The room is preserved and restored, and a visit here is highly recommended. Washington modeled himself after the ancient Roman general Lucius Quinctius Cincinnatus, who after achieving a Roman victory, returned to his farm rather than taking absolute power as a dictator. King George III, after losing the Colonies to the Continental Army, and hearing of Washington's resignation, allegedly declared that his resignation would make him "The greatest man in the world." Plan for 1-2 hours visiting the State House.

• **United States Naval Academy**–No visit to Annapolis would be complete without a visit to the Naval Academy. It is open to the public, but a photo ID is required and hours for visitors may vary (more restrictions may apply during Covid). Be sure to visit the magnificent Naval Academy Chapel, the Statue

• **Mears Marina** is located on Back Creek which is one creek south of Spa Creek. They have 200 slips accommodating boats up to 100 feet. Amenities include pool, tennis courts, picnic areas, and complimentary, continental breakfast in the pavilion every weekend in season. This marina is excellent, but a bit longer walk is required from its Eastport location to go to downtown Annapolis.

Phone: 410-268-8282

Email: desiree@mearsannapolis.com

We suggest staying at least two nights in Annapolis and, if possible, three to enjoy all the sights.

of Tecumseh in front of Bancroft Hall, the obelisk of Herndon, and the Naval Museum that contains the tomb of John Paul Jones. The 90-minute guided tour is the best way to get an introduction to the Academy. Then if you have time, make second visits to sites you enjoyed.

Phone: 410-293-8687 (tours)
121 Blake Road

- **St. John's College**–As noted above, St. John's College is the third oldest college in the United States. It has a sister campus in Santa Fe, New Mexico. It is a 4-year liberal arts college known for its Great Books Curriculum. Together, both campuses have about 770 students. The small, attractive campus is lovely to walk through and is about three blocks from the Paca House.

  Phone: 410-263-2371
  60 College Avenue

- **Hammond-Harwood House Museum**– The Hammond-Harwood House offers a lengthy list of tours that are available by request. Topics range from life in 19th Century Annapolis to in-depth looks at paintings and artists to uncovering hidden treasures on the estate. **https://hammondharwoodhouse.org**.

  Phone: 410-263-4683
  19 Maryland Avenue

- **Woodwind II**–If you would like someone else to man the helm, take a short sail around the Severn River on this classic sailboat that was featured in the 2005 movie, *The Wedding Crashers*. It is tied up on Ego Alley at the Annapolis Waterfront Hotel. Reservations are recommended.

  Phone: 410-263-8994
  80 Compromise Street

- **The Signers Homes**–If you don't mind walking, in a short period of time you can view the homes of all four Maryland signers of the Declaration of Independence. I would start with:

1. **Charles Carroll House of Annapolis**– The Charles Carroll House & Gardens of Annapolis is a beautiful historic waterfront venue on Spa Creek in Historic Downtown Annapolis. Check the website for visitor times. **charlescarrollhouse.org**.

   Email: cchannapolis@gmail.com
   107 Duke of Gloucester Street

2. **Chase Lloyd House & Garden Tours** invites guests to join them for an hour-long tour. The tour will cover architectural details and the longstanding social history that connects these two great houses. By appointment only. **chaselloydhouse.org**.

   Phone: 410-263-4683
   22 Maryland Avenue

3. **William Paca House**–This spectacular Georgian Mansion is owned by the Historic Annapolis Foundation (check **Annapolis.org** for hours of operation) and is a must-see for visitors to Annapolis. The residence and gardens are beautifully restored. It is open to the public.

   Phone: 410-990-4543
   186 Prince George Street

4. **Peggy Stewart House** is a historic house that played a key role in the American Revolution and was home at different times to a signer of the Constitution and a signer of the Declaration of Independence. This private residence is not open to the public.

   207 Hanover Street

EATERIES

Three Historic Inns Downtown

- **Reynolds Tavern**–In 1747, Reynolds Tavern opened as a Tavern and Inn. It changed hands and for a time was a bank, then a library, and is now reborn as a Tavern and Inn once again. Limited accommodations are available. The food is excellent and eclectic.

The 1747 Pub is a charming small gathering spot in the basement.
Phone: 410-295-9555
Email: reynoldstavern@comcast.net
7 Church Street

- **Middleton Tavern** is located at the origin of Ego Alley. The inn and tavern date from 1750. Its famous clientele included the luminaries of the American Revolution; George Washington, Thomas Jefferson, Benjamin Franklin, as well as members of the Continental Congress between 1783-84. See **middletontavern.com** for info on menus and entertainment schedules.
  Phone: 410-263-3323
  2 Market Place

- **Treaty of Paris Inn** on the ground floor of The Maryland Inn. This is one of the most charming restaurants in Historic Annapolis. Lovely overnight accommodations are available at the Maryland Inn.
  Phone: 410-216-6340
  16 Church Street

Other fine restaurants in town include:

- **Café Normandie** serves French country cuisine with Maryland seafood specialties.
  Phone: 410-263-3382
  185 Main Street

- **Carrol's Creek** features fresh local seafood, grilled fish, steaks, chops, soups, and much more!
  Phone: 410-263-8102
  410 Severn Ave (Eastport)

- **Federal House Bar and Grill** is known for its crab soups, burgers, crab cakes, 40+ local craft beers, and an extensive Bloody Mary list.
  Phone: 410-268-2576
  22 Market Space

- **Galway Bay**–Try their famous Fish and Chips, legendary Corned Beef Reuben, one-of-a-kind Shepherd's Pie, or one of their daily specials.
  Phone: 410-263-8333
  63 Maryland Avenue

- **Harry Brown's**
  Phone: 410-263-4332
  63 State Circle

- **Lewnes Steak House**–Its high back booths and low-lit ambiance make Lewnes' a premier spot for special occasions or private dining.
  Phone: 410-263-1617
  401 Fourth Street (Eastport)

- **O'Leary's Seafood**
  Phone: 410-263-0884
  310 Third Street (Eastport)

- **Osteria** is situated amongst the historic buildings that lead to the Bay. Osteria focuses on the taste and passion of Italian coastal cuisine. Original paintings decorate the walls as the glittering chandeliers light the modern art deco style.
  Phone: 410-267-7700
  177 Main Street

- **Ram's Head Restaurant and Show Bar**
  Phone: 410-268-4545
  33 West Street

NEXT DESTINATION: SOLOMONS ISLAND, MARYLAND - 46 Miles

Plan a sunrise deployment for the next stop of Solomon's Island, Maryland that is 46 nautical miles south at the mouth of the Patuxent River.

A model bugeye sailing vessel at the Calvert Marine Museum

Chapter 3
Solomons Island, Maryland
HISTORY

The Island originally was known as Bourne's Island in 1680, then Somervell's Island in1740, and finally Solomon's Island after a 19th Century businessman, Isaac Solomon who established a cannery there in 1865 after the Civil War. Today Solomons Island is known simply as Solomons (the locals drop the irrelevant term Island since there is only an obscure 10-foot roadway bridge that separates the Island from the mainland). Solomons quickly became a fishing and seafood center and a boat-building community. Sailing oyster boats evolved and the most popular type became known as the Chesapeake Bay Skipjack, a one-masted sailboat with shallow draft. Another slightly larger sailboat was the two-masted Bugeye. A few Skipjacks remain on the Bay as historic relics. Other boats from this era were known as Buyboats. These were motorized and would cruise up to the Skipjacks or Bugeyes while at sea and would collect their oyster cargoes and deliver them to port for sale.

During the War of 1812, Commodore Joshua Barney cast off from Solomons to take on the British Frigates on their way up the Patuxent River to burn Washington. Barney's small flo-

built in 1937 by M. M. Davis & Sons' boatyard. The sailing yacht won several races on the Great Lakes including the famous Chicago-Mac race. In 1955, she was donated to the US Coast Guard and converted to a training vessel. While a US Senator, John F. Kennedy saw *Manitou* tied up at the Naval Academy. When Kennedy became president, he ordered the purchase of *Manitou* with the objective of her becoming the Presidential Yacht. Kennedy spent many hours sailing and entertaining on that classic yawl from Solomons.

Solomons played a role in World War II. It was chosen as a training site for amphibious landing exercises in preparation for island attacks in the Pacific Theatre. Ironically, some of those trainees landed at the Solomon Islands in the Pacific.

The Maryland Pilot's Association maintains a house in Solomons for its Bay Pilots who overnight while waiting for or returning from their assigned ship duties.

Solomons is now a popular tourist site.

ARRIVAL BY WATER

When cruising south out of Annapolis, take a course of 160 degrees from Red "4" at Greenbury Point. Honor Green "1AH" at Tolly Point; the shallows extend out to this mark. Then, south at 186 degrees will take you past the famous screw-pile lighthouse at Thomas Point. Get your camera ready; the well-known lighthouse is very picturesque. The mouths of the South River and West River converge in this area. There are fuel docks and safe anchorages in these lovely rivers.

Continue south along a parallel course with the Western Shore of the Bay. You will pass Herring Bay that boasts two lovely marinas with restaurants, fuel docks, activities, and especially Herrington Harbor South. This is one of the largest marinas on the eastern seaboard with 578 slips, good eateries, a pool, and lovely overnight hotel accommodations. They are boater-friendly and, if you have time,

tilla attacked the British at St. Leonard's Creek about 6 miles north of Solomons. They were unable to stop the British who eventually made it to Washington and completed their grisly task. There is no sign or marker of that battle on that Creek. However, it may be worthwhile to visit St. Leonard's Creek, which is a beautiful setting and has many good anchorages. Two miles up the creek is a fun marina known as Vera's White Sands Restaurant and Marina (see notes below).

Until 1940, a former German cruise ship, the *Kronprinzessin Cecilie*, was docked on the western side of Solomons in the Patuxent River. The ship was taken over by the US Navy in 1917, converted to a navy vessel, and carried troops to Europe during World War I. She was renamed *Mount Vernon*. When built in 1907, she was a top-of-the-line cruiser with a length of 706 feet, a gross tonnage of 19,000, and a draft of 31 feet. She was scrapped for metal after 1940.

POINT OF INTEREST

During the 1930s, Solomons was famous for building high-quality pleasure sailing vessels. The most famous was *Manitou*, a 62-foot yawl spend a night. It is 17 nautical miles south of Annapolis. The other marina is Herrington Harbor North, which is more of a working marina with facilities to pull large boats. It is also the home of world-famous Weaver Yachts.

South of Herring Bay, the coast is smooth with easy cruising. About two miles before you arrive at Cove Point you will pass the Calvert Cliffs Nuclear Power Plant, the only nuclear facility in Maryland. It appears only as a white flat top structure off in the distance.

Next, cruising south is the Cove Point Natural Gas Terminal with its long prominent docking pier for large ships that transport liquid natural gas around the world. The tops of five large white holding tanks are visible amidst the trees on shore. Give the loading dock a wide

berth as noted on the chart. Another historic lighthouse, Cove Point Light, built in 1828, is visible at the tip of land at the actual Cove Point. It is the second oldest lighthouse in continuous use in Maryland.

Five miles south of Cove Point is the entrance to the Patuxent River. The Patuxent is said to be the deepest river on the East Coast; at one point to a depth of 122 feet. As you enter the mouth of the River and pass Drum Point to starboard, pay heed to the shallows between Drum Point and the entrance to Mill Creek. I recommend staying to starboard to enter Mill Creek. As you turn to starboard into Mill Creek you will notice a small bulkheaded island to port known as Molly's Leg. As you proceed, you will come upon a fork; stay to port which is Back Creek. This creek gives a boater the best access to the activities of Solomons.

OVERNIGHT

There are many excellent overnight marinas in Solomons. Most prominent is Zahnisers Yachting Center.

• **Zahnisers Yachting Center**– This is a working boat yard with a 75-ton boat lift for large yachts. Zahnisers is known for its quality boat work. It offers slips for overnight, but no fuel. Amenities include a nice gift shop, a fine marine store, and The Dry Dock restaurant on site. There are bicycles for rent and a salt-water pool for transients. All the shops and restaurants of Solomons are within a short walk.
Phone: 410-326-2166

A bit farther up Back Creek is Spring Cove Marina. It has 246 slips, a fuel dock, a pool with a snack bar, bicycles, and a small play area. It is a working boat yard

Sunrise from Zahnisers Marina in Solomons, Maryland

Calvert Marine Museum in Solomons, Maryland

biology or paleontology where you can inspect sharks and other strange sea creatures. They have a wonderful library, a history gallery, gift shop, and opportunities to visit the Lore Oyster House and the Cove Point Lighthouse.

• In addition, you can visit the **Drum Point Lighthouse** next to the Museum and see how the residents of these screw-pile lighthouses lived and maintained the light. You can also take a short cruise on the Buyboat, *Wm. B. Tennison*, and learn about the challenging business of oystering. One could easily spend a full day at this one site.
Phone: 410-326-2042
14200 Solomons Island Road

• **Calvert Cliffs State Park** is about eight miles north of Solomons. It consists of a lengthy, but narrow beach with steep layered cliffs that possess buried fossils from 10 million years ago. It is a popular place to find prehistoric sharks' teeth. Be prepared to take a long walk. Once you park your car and check-in at the Park Ranger's Office you will walk about a mile through a quiet forest to get to the cliffs. Allocate at least half a day for this visit.
Phone: 443-975-4360
10540 H. G. Trueman Road

EATERIES

There are many fine restaurants in Solomons.

• **The Lighthouse Restaurant and Dock Bar**–A lovely restaurant with a grand view of Solomons Harbor. We dined here and the fried shrimp were superb.
Phone: 410-231-2256
14636 Solomons Island Road

and has a 50-ton lift. It is a moderate walk to Solomons, but if you need to buy groceries the owners will help with a rental car.

The historic Cove Point Lighthouse, a 6-mile drive from Solomons, is available for rent on a short or long-term basis. It can accommodate up to 16 people overnight. The lighthouse is also open for day visits. Contact the Calvert Marine Museum for more information.

We suggest staying in Solomons for two nights.

SIGHTS

• **The Calvert Marine Museum**–This active Marine Museum is one of the jewels of Solomons. It has encyclopedic information about the Bay and its history. You can visit the various galleries with displays about estuary

Drum Point Light and the Buyboat, Wm. B Tennison,
(on the left with the tan trim) at Calvert Marine Museum in Solomons

- **The Pier**–Located facing west, the restaurant is the terminus of a 125-foot-long pier with 360-degree views of the water activities.
  Phone: 410-449-8406
  14575 Solomons Island Road

- **Stoney's Kingfisher**–The best crab cakes in Calvert County.
  Phone: 410-394-0236
  14442 Solomons Island Road S

- **The Tiki Bar** is known for its exotic Mai Tai drinks.
  Phone: 410-449-6621
  85 Charles Street

- **Vera's White Sands Restaurant and Marina**–Eight miles north of Solomons by boat on beautiful St. Leonard's Creek. Quirky, Caribbean format, mostly locals, but interesting.
  Phone: 410-586-1182
  1200 White Sands Drive

NEXT DESTINATION: TALL TIMBERS, MARYLAND ON HERRING CREEK

At this point, the cruiser must make a decision. Choice ONE is to bypass the Potomac River and Washington, D.C., and proceed from Solomons to Reedville, Virginia. This cruise is about 38 miles. Choice TWO is to take on the long Potomac River and go to exciting and vibrant Washington, D.C. This choice can be done in one long day if you want to cruise the 120-mile journey — 12 hours underway at 10 knots. It would make sense to split up the trip into two days. I will offer three alternatives for ways to divide the 2-day journey. For some reason, the Potomac River does not have many choices for marinas. But here are my three suggestions.

- **Tall Timbers Marina, Maryland**-From Solomons it is 40 miles. To Washington, it's 75 miles.
  Phone: 301-994-1508
  Email: info@talltimbersmarinasomd.com
- **Cobb Island, Maryland**–From Solomons is 53 miles. To Washington, it's 62 miles.
- **Colonial Beach, Virginia**–From Solomons is 60 miles. To Washington, it's 56 miles.

We decided to take two days to cruise to Washington. We visited Tall Timbers Marina on Herring Creek along the Maryland side of the Potomac to split the trip.

The options of Cobb Island and Colonial Beach will be discussed in subsequent chapters.

Chapter 4
Tall Timbers, Maryland on Herring Creek
HISTORY

The Tall Timbers Marina had its origins in 1920 when "Uncle" Henry Juenemann purchased 132 acres of land around Herring Creek. He liked the tall trees that covered the land and gave it the appellation. There is now a post office of the same name nearby. The creek was a productive oyster ground, and eventually The Reluctant Navigator Restaurant offered the local mollusks for sale. The restaurant has become a popular seafood establishment.

In the 1930s, a boy's summer camp with overnight cabins was located at Tall Timbers. In 1941 the Federal Government needed housing for the newly created Patuxent River Naval Air Base nearby. They took over the boy's camp, which never returned. In 1960, the Army Corps of Engineers dredged the entrance to Herring Creek to a depth of 7 ft and a 60 ft width. This allowed customers to come to the restaurant by water and allowed for larger pleasure craft to overnight at the marina. The working marina, restaurant, beach, and grounds have been owned and operated by one family for over 100 years.

ARRIVAL BY WATER

To get to Tall Timbers from Solomons, repeat your course out into Mill Creek and proceed into the Patuxent heading east. At Green "3" take a course of 121 degrees to Green "1 PR" bell. Head south toward Point No Point Light (52 ft. height). Continue at 191 degrees to Green Can "69A." From there enter the Potomac at 251 degrees to Point Lookout Light that is 39 ft height (you may recall during our discussion under Baltimore that a SeaMaster jet flying boat broke up in mid-air

and crashed in the waters off Point Lookout in December 1955.)

Then take a course of 312 degrees for six miles to Green "SM." This marks the entrance to the St Mary's River and Smith Creek (if you need shelter from severe weather or need fuel there is a marina on Smith Creek to starboard; the Point Lookout Marina). From Green "SM" proceed at 308 degrees for five miles to Red/White "B." Then proceed four miles at 336 degrees. Look to starboard (at about 72 degrees) for square red and green marks on the white, beachy shoreline about a mile away. This is the entrance to Herring Creek and Tall Timbers Marina.

As you enter the narrow channel, stay in the middle and do not turn off until you pass Red "6" at the end of the channel. Turn to starboard and approach the fuel dock at Tall Timbers. The channel averaged a minimum of 7 ft depth with moderate tidal currents.

POINT OF INTEREST

I must mention here one interesting point of historic significance. Just 2.2 miles directly south of the entrance to Herring Creek there is a private blue /white buoy (38° 08' 10" N, 76° 33' 10" W). This buoy is placed there between April 1st and October 31st each year as a marker for divers. Incredibly, this site marks a sunken World War II German U boat! The vessel is U-1105 and the site is maintained by the Institute of Maritime History for the Maryland Historical Trust. In 2001, the site was placed on the National Register of Historic Places. It is Maryland's first historic shipwreck preserve. The U-boat is in good condition on the bottom of the river, despite the US Navy placing an explosive charge on the intact sub in 1949 to sink it. It is available for exploration to experienced divers with permission from the State.

The sub was commissioned on June 3, 1944. It was unique in that it was one of several German submarines that were covered with a layer of experimental synthetic rubber skin to counter Allied sonar devices. This top-secret rubber coating aided the sub in combat conditions and this sub's survival earned it the name "Black Panther." When the War ended in May 1945, the British took possession of the sub, then passed it onto the US Navy for study in 1946. The ship was likely scuttled at this spot in the Potomac because of the 65-foot water depth.

OVERNIGHT AND SITES

• **Tall Timbers** is a family-owned and operated full-service marina. The Reluctant Navigator restaurant is on-site.
Phone: 301-994-1508
Email: info@talltimbersmarinasomd.com
Herring Creek is expansive and beautiful. There are lovely homes that decorate the perimeter. Gulls and blue heron are plentiful. The owner of the marina, Rick, is a kind and bright, old-school gentleman, who greeted us at the fuel dock and assisted us in every way. He was accompanied by his young grandson, Jamison. Rick chatted as the slow diesel pump filled our tanks. He told us about the history of the marina and how busy they were prior to the Covid virus. Unfortunately, the restaurant was closed at this time for lack of business. Rick kindly offered us use of his truck to travel to a local restaurant that remained open. Since we had plenty of victuals onboard, we demurred, but were most grateful.

After we tied up, I explored the grounds of the marina on foot. I was fascinated with the boat yard; it was a scene out of the 1950s. There were many old boats on the hard and in slips, some under cover. Wooden hulled vessels were numerous. Many locals were sanding and painting, hauling vessels, and preparing for fishing on the morrow. The store adjacent to the restaurant was filled with what appeared, to the untrained eye, to be junk. But, alas, with careful inspection, there were innumerable rare boat and engine parts, large and small; some old enough to be antiques. I initiated a brief search for a particular metal slide for my Hatteras but had no luck.

The restaurant was large and accommodating with views of the creek and outdoor picnic tables; but sadly, it was completely empty. A visit to the rest room/shower facilities revealed everything functioning, but no awards would be offered for cleanliness or sparkle.

We had a quiet, delightful meal onboard as the sun set and the water lapped gently on our hull. We had time to watch the clouds and contemplate on this quiet evening. We experienced many beautiful days at sea, and it is wise to stop and observe the beauty of nature immediately before your eyes. The clouds were simultaneously billowing, radiant, reflective, tall, mountainous, and white-black suspended over the gray-blue water. Beautiful reflections undulated on the water. Nature is grand, wonderful, unique, variable, and beautiful. It was rewarding to scan the water and absorb nature's beauty and wonder. Photographs cannot capture the essence.

Welcome to the Tall Timbers Marina.

On this crystal-clear evening, I observed four planets. One hour after sunset, Venus could be seen brightly near the western horizon. About 1.5 hours later one could see the surprisingly prominent orange-red planet, Mars rising in the east. Then, during the middle of the night, in the eastern sky, was another bright planet, Jupiter. With good binoculars and a steady hand, you can see Jupiter's four Galenian moons. On any given night, you may see fewer than four, because they are not visible when in front of or behind the largest planet in our solar system. At this time of year (late summer of 2020), Saturn is visible trailing a few degrees behind (east of) Jupiter. With my binoculars I could not detect the rings.

NEXT DESTINATION: WASHINGTON, D.C. - 75 Miles

Exit Herring Creek following the marks. Once in the Potomac, chart a course of 300 degrees. On my chart, this will take you to Red Nun "10" after 2.4 miles. However, we were unable to locate this buoy. From this point we changed course to 284 degrees and traveled 7 miles to Red/White "C." From here take a course of 311 degrees to Red Green "WR." This marks the entrance to the Wicomico River (Maryland) and as you turn to starboard into the Wicomico, the first point of land on the port side of the river entrance is Cobb Island.

If you choose to skip Tall Timbers and go directly to Cobb Island, see Chapter 5 for Cobb Island directions and details. At the end of that chapter are directions to Washington, D.C.

Chapter 5
Cobb Island, Maryland
HISTORY

The first recorded history of Cobb Island dates back to 1642 when the island was owned by one James Neale, a sea captain who had a reputation for seeking Spanish treasure in the West Indies. The term 'Cobb' comes from the Colonial name for a Spanish dollar coin that was cut into fragments or cobbs and used in pre-revolutionary America as currency. In 1889, George Vickers won the Island in a wager. He established the first permanent homestead on the Island. The one shining moment in its history occurred on December 23, 1900. At Cobb Island, Reginald Fessenden sent and received the first intelligible speech transmission via electromagnetic waves. His experiment was performed using two 50-foot masts one mile apart on the Island.

Annually, in mid-June, a Cobb Island Festival is held that includes an outdoor picnic with musicians, games, and lots of crabs.

ARRIVAL BY WATER

Proceed northwest on a course of 312 degrees from Point Lookout Light Flashing Red "2" at the mouth of the Potomac on the north side. After six miles you will encounter Green "SM." From Green "SM" take a course of 308 degrees for 5.1 miles to Red White "B." From here take a course of 317 degrees toward Ragged Point, VA, and a Flashing Green 44 ft light. From here proceed at 302 degrees for 7.2 miles to Red White "C" off Coltons Point.

Cobb Island, Maryland where the first voice radio transmission was recorded in 1900.

POINT OF INTEREST

If you direct your gaze to starboard toward Coltons Point, there is a small Island of great significance. You will see a lighthouse and a tall white cross. This is St. Clements Island, named after the patron saint of mariners. This Island was chosen by about 200 colonists who sailed on a 4-month journey from the Isle of Wight in England to establish the first European col-

The 40-foot-tall white cross was constructed in 1934 on the 300th anniversary of the landing. The Island for a time was known as Blackstone Island and a lighthouse of that name was constructed in 1850. It was destroyed by fire in 1956. The lighthouse was rebuilt in 2008. The Island is now a State Park, and the state of Maryland now maintains The **St. Clement-Potomac River Museum** on the Island.

St. Clements Island, Maryland, where the first Europeans landed in Maryland in 1634

ony in Maryland on the instructions of Lord Baltimore. This site is considered the birthplace of Maryland. The colonists, including Governor Leonard Calvert, landed here on March 25, 1634, which is now celebrated as Maryland Day. Importantly, Lord Baltimore instructed the colonists to include the first official policy of religious tolerance in America.

Interestingly, the British took possession of this geographically well-positioned Island during both the American Revolution and the War of 1812.

From Red White "C" take a course of 311 degrees, 4.2 miles to Red Green "WR" off Cobb Island to starboard and the mouth of the Wicomico River (Maryland).

Cobb Island consists of about 290 acres, measuring about 1.2 miles in length and .5 mile in width. It is separated from the mainland by Neale Sound. There is a bridge that splits the Island. It has an 18 ft vertical clearance. Enter Neale Sound from the east side via the Wicomico River if your air draft is less than 18 ft.

OVERNIGHT AND SIGHTS

If the wind is not severe, this might be a good place to anchor out for the night. As noted, we elected to overnight at Tall Timbers and did not stay at Cobb Island.

There are two marinas on the east side of the bridge: Rick's on the River with 100 slips with gas, and Shymansky's Marina and Restaurant with 110 slips, gas, and diesel. On the western entrance directly from the Potomac River, there is a dredged channel. The chart notes the depth is five feet, but local knowledge suggests it is less. On the western side of the bridge is one marina, Captain John's Crab House and Marina, with 40 slips and gas (no diesel).

EATERIES

There are many eateries on the Island. All three marinas mentioned have restaurants. Other choices are:

- **Rivah** is known for its gourmet burgers and seafood.
  Phone: 301-259-2879
  12364 Neale Sound Drive

- **Scuttlebutts Bar and Grill**
  Phone: 240-233-3113
  12320 Cobb Island Road

- **Ledo Pizza** has pizza, wings, subs, sandwiches, salads, and more.
  Phone: 301-259-2879
  12364 Neale Sound Drive

- **The Cove at Cobb Island** features locally-roasted and unique coffees, tea, cocoa, and baked goods, with river views. They have events featuring local art and entertainment.
  Phone: 240-233-3318
  12133 Neale Sound Drive

NEXT DESTINATION: WASHINGTON, D.C. - 62 Miles

Our next destination is Washington, D.C. Retrace your course eastward out Neale Sound, past Green "3W" into the Wicomico River, then to Green "1 W" back into the Potomac. Head northwest and follow the circuitous River on its way to our nation's Capital. We go under the 1.6-mile-long Harry W. Nice Bridge (Harry Nice was the 50th Governor of the State of Maryland and served from 1935 to 1939), which is US Route 301. The vertical clearance is 105 feet.

During our cruise in 2020, there was construction under way to build a parallel bridge on the northwest side of the existing bridge. Be cautious as you pass under the bridge and watch for many new buoys, barges, and cranes. Located on the Maryland side, just before passing under the bridge is the huge coal power plant to starboard, the Morgantown Generation Station with its two high smokestacks.

POINT OF INTEREST

Two miles north of the Nice Bridge to starboard is tiny Popes Creek with a small crab house, Captain Billy's, and a restaurant that is known as Gilligan's Pier. But the interesting historic fact about Popes Creek is that it is the place where John Wilkes Booth attempted to escape from Maryland after he assassinated President Abraham Lincoln. Booth and one colleague, David Herold, had departed from the home of Dr. Samuel Mudd, who helped set Booth's fractured leg. Booth's goal was to escape to Virginia, where he felt he would be safe among Southern sympathizers. The distance across the Potomac from Maryland to Virginia here is slightly less than two miles. With the help of a local resident, Thomas

John Wilkes Booth passed through here

The most prominent shipwreck at the Ghost Fleet at Mallow's Bay, Maryland is this steel-hulled ferry boat that ran from Cape Charles, Virginia to Norfolk. Her name was Accomac. She was decommissioned after a fire and deposited at Mallows Bay in 1973.

Jones, Booth and Herold located a small skiff at nearby Dent's Meadow. On the night of April 21, 1865, Booth and Herold set off in total blackness. They became disoriented and turned north and landed a few miles upriver at Cedar Point Neck in Maryland. However, they departed two nights later and correctly navigated across the Potomac to Virginia. But as we recall from our history, Booth's journey to Virginia did not end well.

The Potomac then makes a sharp turn to port, passing the 44-foot light, Green "5" at Mathias Point. The river now courses southwest to Maryland Point Light, with its 42-foot light in the center of the river, after which the river turns to the north again.

POINT OF INTEREST

As we head north close to the Maryland shore, we see an old shipwreck at Red Nun "40" to starboard. This wreck marks Mallows Bay, the home of the "Ghost Fleet" of the Potomac.

In this small Bay are located the remnants of the wooden hulls of more than 100 ships from the World War I era. In addition, there are a few steel-hulled ships. Most of the steel has been salvaged. This "ship graveyard" is home to the largest number of visible historic shipwrecks in the Western Hemisphere. Most of the remnants of the hulls are at water level and are difficult to see from the perspective of the river. The hulls serve as artificial habitats for birds and fish. From the shoreline, kayaks can be launched to see the remnants of the hulls. The area is too shallow for large boats. Mallows Bay is a public park with water access and a small boat launch.

We visited later by land and it is a worthwhile excursion if you have a kayak. Also, guided kayak tours are available on Sundays with reservations. Kayak rentals are included in the price of the tour. Go to **Charlescounty.com** and type in Mallows Bay to make a reservation.

Mt. Vernon, Virginia

The Capital Wheel at National Harbor, Maryland

We pass Quantico, Virginia to port (see the section below under departure from Washington, D.C. for more details on Quantico). Just beyond Quantico is a large factory-like structure that is the Possum Point Power Station. Here the River begins to narrow and turn northeast.

Occoquan Bay, Virginia is next on the port side. To starboard is the town of Indian Head, Maryland. Stay to the deeper Maryland side of the River and follow the marks. There is a large sandbar to port as you pass Occoquan Bay. Observe the marks carefully. The River turns north again and then northeast. Fort Belvoir is just north of Red "64." This is a restricted area.

The home of George Washington, Mt Vernon is ahead to port near Green Mark "71" (visiting Mt. Vernon by boat is outlined below after departing from Washington). As you get closer to Alexandria, you will see the Woodrow Wilson Bridge that connects Alexandria, Virginia with Maryland.

The Buried Steel Man at National Harbor, Maryland

Before reaching the Wilson Bridge, to starboard is the National Harbor Marina with 71 slips. The huge Ferris wheel known as the Capital Wheel is at the end of the Marina Pier and is the most prominent sight as you approach. National Harbor is not simply a marina, but rather a waterfront resort, with seven fabulous hotels, along with innumerable restaurants and shops. This is an alternative place to overnight on your boat with easy access to Alexandria and Washington by cab or Uber.

We stayed here for one night. As you enter the open harbor be sure to honor the Red daymark "2" and Green Flashing "3." This channel runs very close to the land on the starboard side. If you draw more than three feet, you should pay particular attention to the marks and buoys, all the way to the docks. The Marina has floating docks and gas and diesel are available.

Besides shops and restaurants, there is a playground and carousel for children. A sandy area with what appears to be a large partially buried steel man is an interesting attraction. Next to that is an outdoor theater screen. The area is vibrant and fascinating with many visitors by land and water.

Chapter 6
Washington, D.C.
HISTORY

In terms of east coast Colonial cities, Washington, D.C. is relatively new. It was officially founded on July 16, 1790. You will recall Annapolis was founded in 1649 and re-named in 1694, while Baltimore was founded in 1706. Washington is unique for several reasons. It was created by the US Constitution under Article I, Section 8, clause 17, as a Federal City. The Federal Government maintains control over the District of Columbia, and it has no voting representatives in the US Congress as the states do. The District has local executive, legislative, and judicial branches pursuant to the Home Rule Act of 1973. However, it is still subject to the US Congress.

When the District was established in 1790, both Virginia and Maryland agreed to make property donations to the 10-mile x 10-mile plot of land on the Potomac River. There are concrete obelisks planted in the ground at the four corners of the square outlining the points of the District of Columbia. In addition, obelisks were planted every mile along each of the four straight sides. Of the 40 installed, 36 can still be found.

In 1791, President George Washington appointed Pierre L'Enfant to design a layout for the new Capital city. L'Enfant's plan included a 400-foot-wide grand avenue (now the Mall) and boulevards to connect Congress House (the Capital) with the President's House (the White House). Included in his plan was a canal system connecting the Potomac and Anacostia Rivers.

Washington eventually dismissed L'Enfant over disagreements about the details of the plan raised by Andrew Ellicott, a local land surveyor, who eventually completed the city plans.

Soon, construction began for the original federal buildings that included the Capital, the Library of Congress, and the White House.

The most dramatic event in the Capital's early history was the attack and burning of federal buildings during the War of 1812 as described above in the section on Baltimore. The losses included the White House, the Capital, and the Library of Congress. No private homes or buildings were destroyed by the British in the Capital. The lost books in the Library of Congress were partially replaced by Thomas Jefferson in 1815 when he sold his valuable library to the government.

The other less well-known part of the attack on Washington involved the British war ships that sailed up the Potomac River. While Admiral Cockburn was preparing to advance up the Patuxent River toward Washington, the one-legged Captain James Gordon was preparing his fleet of seven capital ships to proceed up the Potomac River to attack the American Capitol from the water. The Potomac River was circuitous, winding, and known for its

The tallest obelisk in the world is the Washington Monument, standing 555 feet tall.

many shallows and shoals that were poorly documented in that era. One other obstacle to war ships was a well-placed fort on the Maryland side about 12 miles south of the Capital. Fort Warburton, now known as Fort Washington, was ideally set on bluffs at one of the narrowest points in the Potomac, only 900 yards in width. And the deep channel is close to the Maryland side and is only about 100 yards wide. Enemy ships operated at a distinct disadvantage.

British Captain Gordon sailed up the Potomac on August 17, 1814, the same day Admiral Cockburn departed up the Patuxent River. They both had the same objective. Captain Gordon soon encountered difficulties. Several of his ships ran aground on the Kettle Bottom Shoals just south of Cobb Island near the mouth of the Wicomico River. Despite sending small boats ahead, more of Gordon's ships ran aground. Finally, good breezes appeared, and they were able to sail to Maryland Point where tidal changes required them to anchor on August 24th. This was the night that the other arm of the British attack burned the Capital. Gordon and his sailors could see the glow of the fires on the northern horizon and realized that Admiral Cockburn and General Ross had completed their task. Nonetheless, Captain Gordon decided to sail on to Washington. That evening they were hit by heavy rains and high winds, the same storm that helped douse the flames in the Capitol. On August 26th, they passed Mt. Vernon and, unbelievably, saluted General Washington's home with the band playing "Washington's March. "

As they approached Fort Warburton with trepidation, they were surprised when no shots were fired from the fort and they passed without disturbance.

Fort Washington, Maryland

return down the Potomac would not be as easy as his arrival.

Local American Continental troops, smarting and upset over the defeat at Bladensburg and the burning of the Capital, along with militia from Maryland and Virginia gathered to harass the British as they sailed down the Potomac. The old family homesite of Sally Fairfax, Belvoir (now Fort Belvoir) was used as a base for cannon placement to fire on Gordon's fleet. Although Gordon's departure was punctuated by cannon and musket fire from both shores of the Potomac, by September 9, 1814, he arrived safely back in the Chesapeake Bay.

Incidentally, the final skirmish of the War of 1812 on the Chesapeake Bay occurred on February 7, 1815. It was known as the "Battle of the Ice Mound" and occurred off the shores of Taylor Island near the mouth of the Little Choptank River. A British tender with 18 men aboard from the *HMS Dauntless* invaded some farms on Taylor Island and took off two servants and seven sheep. While sailing away they became caught up in freezing ice drifts. When the local militia was called out, they walked out on the ice and found protection behind mounds of ice. They began firing on the unmovable tender. After a 2-hour standoff, the British surrendered and the day was saved.

The forts commanding officer, Captain Samuel Dyson had 57 men and 3,000 pounds of gunpowder providing many guns and shots. For reasons unclear, he spiked the guns, burned the powder, and departed. He was later court-martialed and dismissed from the army.

On Sunday, August 28, 1814, Captain Gordon arrived at Alexandria, while smoke still drifted from the burned Federal Buildings across the Potomac River. The Alexandria Mayor, Charles Simms, negotiated with Captain Gordon and acceded to his demands. Gordon looted Alexandria of flour, tobacco, cotton, wine, sugar, coffee, and of course, cigars. His

The War of 1812 ended with the Treaty of Ghent, signed on December 24, 1814. The hugely important Battle of New Orleans, where the British were crushed, occurred on January 8, 1815; after the Treaty was signed. This Battle victory made Andrew Jackson a national hero and propelled him to the presidency in 1829.

After the War of 1812, the Federal City continued to grow, and, by the time of the Civil War (1861-1865), it was a busy metropolis. As a Federal City, not beholden to any state, the slaves of the city were freed nine months before the Emancipation Proclamation of April 16, 1862. Washington, D.C. became a haven for slaves during and after the Civil War. There were many job opportunities and new high schools, and colleges were opened for African-Americans, including Howard University in 1867. The Capital city became home to a significant and vibrant black population.

African Americans held many positions in the Federal Government until the administration of President Woodrow Wilson (1912-1921). Wilson watched over the segregation of the Federal bureaucracy during his administration.

Not only is there no Senator or House member from the Federal City, but there was no mayor until 1973. Citizens were first allowed to vote in a Presidential election in 1964.

Today, Washington houses most of the Federal Government's three Branches and hosts many embassies making it a cosmopolitan city with fine hotels, restaurants, and of course, innumerable sights for visitors.

Of historic interest, four US presidents successfully were assassinated while serving in office. Two of those assassinations occurred in Washington, D.C. The first was Abraham Lincoln on April 14, 1865 at the terminus of the Civil War. His murder occurred in Ford's Theatre, which is now a National Historic Site. Performances are still carried out in the theatre and there are guided tours for the public. Incidentally, Lincoln survived a prior assassination attempt in April 1864. He was riding alone at night in Washington when a shot rang out and a bullet struck his tall hat. The culprit was never found.

The second presidential assassination was that of James Garfield, who was shot in the back on July 2, 1881 at the Baltimore & Potomac Railroad Station in Washington. He had served only six months as president and was unique for having no interest in procuring the office. He died from complications of the bullet wound on September 19, 1881.

The other two presidents who were assassinated while in office were William McKinley in Buffalo, New York (September 6, 1901) and John F. Kennedy in Dallas, Texas (November 22, 1963).

ARRIVAL BY WATER

POINT OF INTEREST

As you cruise up the Potomac toward Washington, Red Nun "76" marks the entrance to the shallow Piscataway Creek to starboard. On the creek's north shore, on a low hill, is a large brick and mortar structure, Fort Warburton, now Fort Washington. It is difficult to imagine how Colonel Dyson could leave this well-positioned and well-fortified fort when British Captain Gordon approached with his small fleet. Had Dyson fired from the fort, Captain Gordon in all likelihood would have been turned back and Alexandria would have been saved. Fort Washington was expanded after the War of 1812 and several times through World War II. It is now a 300-acre public park and is worth a visit by land. There are no docks for tying up.

As you pass under the Wilson Bridge, the historic Colonial city of Alexandria, Virginia is to port. There is one small marina, the Alexandria City Marina which has 63 slips. Reservations are recommended and they have only 30-amp power. There are many new apartments and condos along the newly developed waterfront of Alexandria.

As you pass the charming waterfront city of Alexandria, you will notice the many passenger jets zooming overhead. They are using the Ronald Reagan Washington National Airport just ahead to port. At the level of the airport, the Potomac River splits into three waterway alternatives. To port, the Potomac continues

The view from the Washington Channel as one approaches the nation's Capital.

to starboard. Once secured in your slip you can spend many hours walking along the waterfront and enjoy the sights and sounds of the Nation's Capital.

OVERNIGHT

As you enter the Washington Channel, to starboard is the Gangplank Marina.

• **Gangplank Marina** has been rebuilt and now has 300+ slips with floating docks, but no fuel.
Phone: 202-554-5000

• **Capital Yacht Club** with its 88 slips dedicated to full-time residents and several more for transient yachts. It is a fine place to overnight if your yacht club reciprocates.
Phone: 202-488-8110
Email: office@capitalyachtclub.com

Reservations are required for any overnight stays at the Gangplank Marina or the Capital Yacht Club along this newly developed coastline. We stayed at the Capital Yacht Club with its friendly staff and members.

The one-half mile of new hotels, condos, shops, restaurants, and entertainment has enhanced the Washington waterfront. This area is now known as The Wharf.

SIGHTS

Washington D.C. likely has more sights to see than any metropolitan area in America. The length of your stay in Washington is the critical factor controlling what you will have time to see. I would recommend a minimum of three days/nights. Ideally, five days/night would make the most sense. I will lay out a plan for a five-day visit with diminishing priorities as the

into downtown Washington, but bridges obstruct the trip unless your air draft is less than 18 feet. To starboard is the Anacostia River that is more commercial. The central channel is known as the Washington Channel. It has the most choices for overnight boaters.

Distractions abound as you cruise at No Wake speed beyond the Wilson Bridge. Besides jets busily landing and taking off, one can easily see in the distance to the north the elegant obelisk, the Washington Monument. The US Capital Dome, with Liberty atop, stands out in the skyline. Stay on course into the Washington Channel and tie up at one of the great marinas days pass. So, if you can stay only three days, hit those spots listed first.

Travel within Washington is relatively easy. The underground Metro system is quite good and can place you within easy walking distance of any of the major sights. The nearest station to The Wharf is the Waterfront Station on the Green Line, about a half-mile walk.

Incidentally, all national museums in Washington are free.

PROPOSED SCHEDULE

On your arrival day, after tying up and getting plugged in, spend the afternoon and evening exploring by foot the many shops and restaurants along the Wharf area.

Day 1–Morning:

- **Washington Monument** is a recommended visit. There will be a wait to take the elevator to the top, but the view is spectacular. This is the tallest structure in Washington.

Allocate half a day, but you may be able to reduce that time if you get an early start. Hours of operation are 9:00 a.m. to 5:00 p.m. It is best to order tickets in advance.

Afternoon:

- **Smithsonian Air and Space Museum** is one of the most popular spots in Washington.

The exhibits are too vast to describe and even difficult to absorb in person. The museum attempts to document man's experience with flight, from the Wright brothers to manned space flight. Do not miss this museum. Allocate at least half a day. Hours are 10:00 a.m. to 5:30 p.m.
Phone: 202-633-2214
655 Jefferson Drive SW

Day 2–Morning:

- **White House** tour. This must be planned. Tickets are obtained from your Congressional House Representative. Three-month requests are wise, but you can try no less than 21 days before your visit. If you can get tickets it is worth it. Allocate half a day.

Afternoon:

- Visit the **National Archives Museum** to view the Declaration of Independence and the US Constitution. Plan half a day including a walk from the White House.
700 Pennsylvania Avenue NW

Day 3–Morning:

- **Lincoln Memorial**–All outdoors, but impressive. Nearby are the Cherry Blossom Trees that bloom in late March through early April. Allocate two hours.

Afternoon:

- Walk to the nearby **Vietnam Memorial** and with another short walk to see the World War II Memorial. The Martin Luther King, Jr Memorial is not far by foot. Estimate two hours.

- With some time remaining, visit the **Jefferson Memorial** which is near The Wharf. One hour should be enough. When we visited the Jefferson Memorial it was getting a face-lift, but was still open for tourists.

Day 4–Morning:

- **International Spy Museum** has fascinating stuff and there is a nice gift shop with some interesting books. You can even go undercover and test your spy skills on a mission as you travel the Museum's permanent exhibitions. Your performance is tracked and you receive a debrief upon conclusion. Set aside about half a day.
Phone: 202-393-7798
700 L'Enfant Plaza SW

Afternoon:

- Visit the **US Capital Building**–Guided tours are excellent and although tickets are available daily it is best to order tickets in advance. You may be able to say hello to your Representative or Senator, depending on how busy they are. You should be able to do the tour in half a day.

- If you have time you can walk behind the Capital Building across the street and see the **US Supreme Court**. Self-guided tours are available. The Northwest door on the left side under the steps is open from 7:30 a.m. until 4:30 p.m. The Southwest door is on the right side under the steps and is open from 9:00 a.m. to 3:00 p.m.

Day 5–Morning:

- **National Museum of African American History & Culture** is the only national museum devoted exclusively to the documentation of African American life, history, and culture. The museum has collected more than 36,000 artifacts with three floors of exhibits. Suggest half a day.
Phone: 844-750-3012
1400 Constitution Avenue NW

Afternoon:

- **Visit Georgetown** with its shops and excellent restaurants. If time allows you should walk through the historic **Georgetown University**. Half a day should be enough time.
Phone: 202-687-0100
37th and O Streets NW

ALTERNATIVES

- **The Library of Congress** offers several programs and multiple options of ways to access their incredible collections.
101 Independence Avenue SE

- **Arlington National Cemetery**–See Kennedy's grave with the eternal flame. This site, with its beautiful home on the hill, was the residence of General Robert E. Lee.

- **Ford's Theatre**–Where President Abraham Lincoln was shot. Reserve tickets in advance. Tour is two hours.
Phone: 202-347-4833
511 10th Street NW

- **Kennedy Center**–See if a show is in town.
Phone: 202-416-8000
2700 F Street NW

- **Holocaust Museum**–The Museum is free and open six days a week. It is closed on Wednesdays, Yom Kippur, and Christmas Day. Check for current times.
Phone: 202-488-0400
100 Raoul Wallenberg Place SW

- **National Theatre**–See if a show is in town
1321 Pennsylvania Avenue NW

If you like to see colleges, visit the lovely campus of the **University of Maryland** at College Park, Maryland. The Metro Green Line will take you there. Georgetown University is a few subway stops away from the Wharf.

There are many bus tour companies in Washington. The Big Bus Tour company offers tours to most of the spots mentioned above using a "hop on, hop off" alternative.

EATERIES

The number of top restaurants in Washington is too numerous to count. Here are a few:

- **The Grill**–Located on the Wharf; start at your home dock.
Phone: 202-916-5996
99 Market Street SW

- **Del Mar** is known for its fine Spanish-style seafood.
Phone: 202-525-1402
791 Wharf Street SW

- **ABC Pony Burger & Fries**–Choose from the menu or build your own. Open Tuesday-Saturday 11:00 a.m.-10:00 p.m.
  Phone: 202-913-8155
  21st Street SE

- **Mekki DC**–True Moroccan cuisine.
  Phone: 202-525-5472
  517 8th Street SE

- **Café Riggs**–Inspired by the bustling brasseries of Europe, Café Riggs offers traditional grace through a re-imagined lens to bring a modern restaurant to Washington, D.C.
  Phone: 202-638-1800
  900 F Street NW

- **Seasons Restaurant** in the Four Seasons Hotel. A fine steak house.
  Phone: 202-944-9151
  2800 Pennsylvania Ave NW

- **Old Ebbitt Grill**–History goes back to 1856, it has great food and an oyster bar.
  Phone: 202-347-4800
  675 15th Street SW

NEXT DESTINATION: COLONIAL BEACH, VIRGINIA - 56 Miles

As we travel south along the Potomac, we will concentrate on sights on the Virginia side of the River. The trip to Colonial Beach, Virginia is 56 nautical miles from Washington, D.C. Retrace your entrance out of the Washington Channel and down the Potomac River. About 30 minutes after departure you will arrive at Mt. Vernon, Virginia, some 11 miles south. There is a deep-water channel to cruise into Mt. Vernon and a large commercial pier for tour boats. The channel is well marked with Red "2" at the channel entrance. If you desire to visit Mt. Vernon and the George Washington Tomb, you should call ahead to confirm you may tie up at the dock. Mt. Vernon is open 365 days a year (yes, including holidays) from 9:00 a.m. to 4:00 p.m.

At approximately 27 miles south of Washington D.C., you will see to starboard the town of Quantico, Virginia, which includes the Marine Corps Base Quantico. This Marine Base houses about 12,000 military and civilian personnel and is home to the Marine Corps Officer Candidate School. It is also home to the Drug Enforcement Administration and the FBI Academy. There is no public access by boat.

You have another 29 miles to Colonial Beach, Virginia. Two miles south of the Harry Nice Bridge on the Virginia side you will see the town of Dahlgren, Virginia. Located here, since 1918, is a Naval Base named after Admiral John Dahlgren. For a time in the 1970s, it was known as the Naval Surface Weapons Center and was a test site for small rockets. Research for the defensive AEGIS missile system was developed here. In 2006, it was renamed the "Naval Support Activity-South Potomac. "

Chapter 7
Colonial Beach, Virginia
HISTORY

Colonial Beach was originally named "The Point" in 1651. George Washington was born near here in 1732 as was James Monroe in 1758. After Colonial times the town developed into a fishing resort. The town was incorporated in 1893 as Colonial Beach and construction of houses, summer cottages and hotels began. Most people arrived by boat from Washington, D.C. Alexander Graham Bell built a summer house here that still stands as the Bell House Bed and Breakfast. By the late 19th Century Colonial Beach was known as the "Playground of the Potomac." After the Chesapeake Bay Bridge opened in 1952, automobile traffic redirected toward the Eastern Shore beaches and Colonial Beach dwindled. For a brief period, the town became known for gambling and slot machines because of a quirk in the state law. Maryland allowed gambling from 1949 to 1958 and the Maryland state line extended to the low water mark of Virginia's Potomac River shore. Pier casinos were extended over the state line into Maryland and until 1958 gambling gave the local economy a boost. At the beach front restaurant known as Riverboat on the Potomac, gambling is still allowed because it extends into Maryland waters.

In 2019, Colonial Beach was designated The Nicest Place in Virginia" by USA Today.

ARRIVAL BY WATER

Three miles after the mid-river Red/White "D" mark, head south toward Red "2" and into the narrow channel with Red "4" at the opening of the 6-foot-deep channel which enters Monroe Creek.

As noted above in Chapter 3, Colonial Beach could be used as a stop when cruising from Solomons to Washington. The trip from Solomons is 60 miles, making this point almost exactly the halfway point between Solomons and Washington.

OVERNIGHT

- We recommend staying at **Colonial Beach Yacht Center** with 150 slips. Amenities include gas/diesel, water, electricity, pumpout, Wi-Fi, a marine store, picnic areas, restaurant, and a private beach. This marina is immediately to starboard as you enter Monroe Creek.
Waypoint: 38° 13' 47"N / 76° 57' 45"W
Phone: 804-224-7230
Email: mail@cbycmarina.com

SIGHTS

Golf carts are available to drive to local attractions. There are many restaurants, inns,

The former summer home of
Alexander Graham Bell in Colonial Beach, Virginia

and shops to see along the 2-mile Potomac River beach.

Stratford Hall is about 10 miles south. It is the birthplace of Gen. Robert E. Lee and the longtime home of the Lee family. The birthplace of George Washington is about four miles south and James Monroe's birthplace is about two miles from Colonial Beach.

EATERIES

• **Dockside Restaurant and Tiki Bar** is next to the marina. You can dine in by candlelight, by the fireplace in the pub, on the screened-in porch, in the sand at their picnic tables, or at the tiki bar.
Phone: 804-224-8726
1787 Castlewood Drive

• **Lenny's Restaurant** specializes in Philly-style cheesesteaks and submarine sandwiches.
Phone: 804-224-9675
301 Colonial Avenue

• **Lighthouse Restaurant** serves American, seafood, and sushi. A family-owned and operated restaurant that for decades has been serving fresh and healthy All-American food. They offer many daily specials.
Phone: 804-224-7580
11 Monroe Bay

NEXT DESTINATION: REEDVILLE, VIRGINIA - 55 Miles

The next leg of our journey will take us down the Potomac River to its mouth and south around Smith Point to Reedville, Virginia. The town is located on a small creek off the Great Wicomico River, Cockrell Creek. An alternate course is to skip Reedville and go straight to the Rappahannock River to Irvington, Virginia on Carter Creek. This adds mother 23 miles to the journey for a total of 78 miles from Colonial Beach. We elected to stay for one night in Reedville.

Chapter 8
Reedville, Virginia
HISTORY

Captain Elijah Reed arrived in the Northern Neck of Virginia in 1874. He had come from Maine to fish for menhaden and extract oil from them efficiently. The remnants of the menhaden were useful for fertilizer. By 1885, the town was known as Reedville and was heavily engaged in the menhaden fishing industry. The 500 residents became quite wealthy and Reedville was once known as the wealthiest town in America. Today, one can visit the Millionaire's Row of Victorian mansions in the downtown Historic District. The Omega Protein Corporation with several hundred employees, remains very busy in the menhaden business. Tyson Foods is a substantial customer using the menhaden protein additive for poultry feed.

The Omega Protein Corporation in the background in Reedville, Virginia. The blue-hulled menhaden fishing boats are in the foreground.

ARRIVAL BY WATER

Six miles south of Smith Point is Red Nun "2" that marks the entrance to the Great Wicomico River. As you enter the River you will see Red "4" and Red "6." Honor both of these to avoid the shallows. Be on the lookout for many floats of crab pots. Keep to starboard to enter Cockrell Creek. In approximately two miles you will see a tall chimney. Across the creek from this landmark is the Fairport Marina and Restaurant. Farther along the creek is the Reedville Marina with 19 slips for boats under 30 feet. The Crazy Crab Restaurant is located at the Marina. Both were closed due to Covid.

We saw several menhaden fishing vessels in port at the Omega Factory. They are characterized by their blue hulls and 130 ft length.

OVERNIGHT

• We stayed at the **Fairport Marina** on Cockrell Creek. They have 48 slips with a fuel dock and electric. Amenities include water, Wi-Fi, pump-out, ship store, and showers. Call in advance to confirm the availability of slips. This marina is located across the creek from the Omega Plant and to our surprise the plant stayed open all night with bright lights and faint background noise. We still slept well.
Waypoint: 37.83308° N / 76.28613° W
Phone: 804-543-5002

SIGHTS

The center of town is about a 2-mile walk from the Fairport Marina.

• In town, there is the **Reedville Fishermen's Museum** that has two skipjacks and many displays about the menhaden industry. The museum's mission is to acquire, document, interpret, and display materials that are historically important to the lower Chesapeake Bay with special emphasis on activities relating to Reedville fisheries and the lives of the region's watermen, and to establish educational programs to interpret this maritime heritage.
Phone: 804-453-6529
504 Main Street

You can take a walk along Millionaire's Row. From Reedville, there is a small cruise ship available that will take passengers to visit historic Tangier Island 17 miles away in the center of the Chesapeake Bay.

EATERIES

• **The Crazy Crab**–Seafood and American cuisine on the water.
Phone: 804-453-6789
902 Main Street

• **Reedville Market**–Seafood and steaks in a nice waterfront setting. Other options such as the crab cake sandwich, French dip, tuna sashimi, cheeseburgers, wings, quesadillas, and pasta.
Phone: 804-453-4666
729 Main Street

We ended up dining on the boat since the restaurants had restricted opening times.

A mansion in the background along Millionaire's Row in Reedville, Virginia

NEXT DESTINATION: IRVINGTON, VIRGINIA - 32 Miles

Irvington, Virginia is a quaint town on beautiful Carter Creek, on the north shore of the Rappahannock River. We planned to stay at a well-known hotel and marina, the Tides Inn.

Chapter 9
Irvington, Virginia
HISTORY

It appears that the early settlers who came to the Irvington area on Carter Creek were fishermen from the Eastern Shore of Maryland. They continued their life as watermen. There were few roads in that era and most activities were carried out by boat. The town of Irvington was established in 1891. It was named after a popular local sea captain, Levin H. Irvington. A steamboat landing was built at the mouth of Carter Creek to accommodate boats from Baltimore and other ports. Irvington expanded as a steamboat town during the 1890s and grew along with the adjacent towns of White Stone to the east and Kilmarnock to the north. A fire severely damaged the town in 1917. As steamboats went out of business and automobiles and roads expanded, Irvington declined.

The entrance of the famous Tides Inn at Irvington, Virginia

The Tides Inn at Irvington, Virginia

service was used for vehicular traffic.

ARRIVAL BY WATER

After departing Reedville and out the Great Wicomico River look for Green "C3" at the mouth and head south. From here Windmill Point Light, a 34-foot mark, is 12 miles. Enter the Rappahannock River. The Norris Bridge is 9.5 miles from Windmill Point Light; vertical clearance is no problem at 110 ft. Two miles beyond the Bridge, to starboard is the entrance to Carter Creek with Red "2" marking the entrance. Two more miles to starboard is the Tides Inn and Marina.

OVERNIGHT

• The **Marina at Tides Inn** has floating docks that can accommodate up to 24 vessels up to 150 feet. Gas and diesel are available. Overnight guests at the marina have full use of the resort's amenities. The amenities include electric, pump-out, a bag of ice, water, cable TV, wireless internet service, newspapers, local phone calls, use of the Par 3 golf course, lawn and beach games, shuttle service to the Golden Eagle Golf Club and the town of Kilmarnock, laundry facilities, climate-controlled showers, use of the Tides Inn's bicycles, fitness center, paddleboards, kayaks, paddleboats, and canoes. Reservations for overnight stays at the Marina are recommended. If there are no slips available, there are several other marinas on Carter Creek.

Phone: 804-438-4418
Email: marina@tidesinn.com

After World War II, Americans became more mobile, and tourism helped revitalize Irvington after the Tides Inn Hotel was constructed in 1947. The lovely property overlooking Carter Creek was an ideal location for the 47-room resort developed by E. A. Stevens. Soon a golf course and a marina adorned the resort and recently Travel & Leisure labeled Tides Inn as one of the "Top Resorts in the Continental United States." Tides Inn and Marina is now part of the Enchantment Resort Group.

Prior to 1957, when the Norris Bridge was built across the Rappahannock River, ferry boat

The Hope and Glory Inn at Irvington, Virginia

SIGHTS

Irvington has many worthwhile sights. They include:

ART GALLERIES

• **Objects, Art, and More** houses fine art, paintings, sculpture, jewelry, pottery, glass, wood, and metal sculptures from a wide variety of artists and genres.
Phone: 804-438-8024
4462 Irvington Road

• **Dog and Oyster Vineyard**– Owner-Hosted Private Tastings at the Hope and Glory Inn can be arranged any day of the week.
Phone: 804-761-7879
170 White Fences Drive

• **Bay Aviation Airplane Rides** flies out of Hummel Airfield which is about a 15-minute drive from the marina. For less than $150 you can spend 30 minutes in the air viewing the spectacular scenery from an open cockpit, single-engine PT-19 Warbird airplane. Beautiful.
Phone: 804-436-2977
2649 Greys Point Road

• **Steamboat Era Museum**–It tells the story of the steamboats and how they altered the lives of everyone along the Chesapeake Bay. The era is brought to life with models, artifacts, and photos. Here you can step back in time, back to a romantic time full of adventure, splendor, and prosperity.
Phone: 804-438-6888
156 King Carter Drive

EATERIES

• **The Tides Inn**–There are five restaurant choices for excellent food at the Inn:
Phone: 804-438-5000
480 King Carter Drive

• **Chesapeake Restaurant & Terrace**– Where New England seafood meets southern comfort.

• **Fish Hawk Oyster Bar** is a casual, coastal eatery at the Tides Inn featuring indoor and outdoor seating along Carter Creek. Grab-and-go seafood favorites and an indoor raw bar.

- **Eagle Room** represents the Inn's storied past and is outfitted with vintage Bourbon lockers and anchored by a large, hand-carved wooden eagle.

- **Golden Eagle Grill**–Located at the Golden Eagle Golf Club, guests can enjoy light American fare before heading out on the golf course or following a successful morning on the greens.
  Phone: 804-438-4460
  364 Clubhouse Road

- **Overlook Dining**–Eat under the trees. Reservations are required.
  Phone: 804-438-4489
  480 King Carter Drive

- **The Hope & Glory Inn**–A true dining experience. This 1890 building was a schoolhouse and in 1996 was converted into an Inn with a tiny but superb restaurant.

Reservations are required. Breakfast and dinner. Definitely worth the experience.
Phone: 804-438-6053
65 Tavern Road

- **The Dredge**–They source most of their produce and also raise their own grass-fed cattle, pigs, and chickens at their family-owned "Black Sheep Farm" in Lively, Virginia.
  Phone: 804-438-6363
  4357 Irvington Road

- **The Office Café**–A fresh American bistro with full bar service for lunch and dinner. All freshly prepared from scratch using locally sourced ingredients, fresh seafood, and artfully prepared desserts.
  Phone: 804-438-8032
  4346 Irvington Road

I would recommend staying two nights at the marina to have time for all the sights and activities.

NEXT DESTINATION: YORKTOWN, VIRGINIA - 44 Miles

Our next destination is historic Yorktown on the beautiful York River. The trip from Carter Creek is 44 miles. Follow your track out of Carter Creek into the Rappahannock River and under the Norris Bridge. At 11 miles out of Carter Creek, you will encounter R "3." Leave this mark to starboard and swing south past Stingray Point Light with its 34-foot tower. Continue south past the wide Mobjack Bay to the entrance of the York River. Look for R "14" and turn to starboard into the River's mouth. There is a shoal that extends out three miles from Guinea Neck and honoring R "14" will take you safely past.

Chapter 10
Yorktown, Virginia
HISTORY

Yorktown was founded in 1691 as a deep-water port on the York River. It was named after the ancient city of York in Northern England. It was known as "York" until after the American Revolution when "Yorktown" came into common usage. By 1750 it had a population of about 2,000. It is a good port because the water depth at the shoreline drops off to 70 feet. The channel between Yorktown and Gloucester Point is deep water across its entire width. There is a substantial current of three knots or more.

Yorktown became famous during the American Revolution. It was here that the last major battle of the Revolution occurred. After this crushing defeat, the British lost their will to fight and American Independence was assured. During the summer of 1781, British General Charles Cornwallis moved his army north through the Carolinas and decided on taking a position at Yorktown. As a good port, the town would offer a means of escape, if necessary, utilizing the British fleet that was based in New York. However, the French fleet under Admiral François de Grasse sailed from the Santo Domingo to the mouth of the Chesapeake Bay and blocked the British fleet from rescuing Cornwallis. Under the Marquis de Lafayette, the American army surrounded Cornwallis in Yorktown. Washington and additional troops arrived at Yorktown and a siege began which lasted from October 9-17, 1781. After eight days of persistent bombardment, and no chance of rescue by sea, Cornwallis and his 7,000 troops surrendered on October 19, 1781. After this stunning defeat, the British crown elected to cut their losses, and the American Revolution ended with victory when the Treaty of Paris was signed in Annapolis, on January 14, 1784. One other notable American fought at Yorktown. That was Alexander Hamilton, who became the first Secretary of the Treasury in the Washington Administration.

Yorktown was involved in another battle, this time during the Civil War. The Union Army, under General George McClellan, planned to attack the Confederate Capital, Richmond, Virginia. The Union Army, consisting of 120,000 men, was transported by ships to Fort Monroe at Hampton, Virginia. McClellan had planned to attack Yorktown by sea, but the historic Battle of Hampton Roads (March 8-9, 1862) caused him to modify his plans. This sea battle was the first of its kind between "iron-clad" ships, the Merrimac for the South, and the Monitor for the North. The battle was a draw, but McClellan decided to invade by land rather than by sea. With his huge army, McClellan marched up the peninsula (April 5-May 4, 1862) where he first encountered the Confederate forces at Yorktown under General John Magruder. Magruder had only 12,000 troops, but he created a defensive line across the peninsula, the Warwick Line. Magruder even used some of the remnants of Cornwallis' trenches still in place from the 1781 battle. After a one-month engagement at Yorktown, Magruder was pushed back to Williamsburg. After a brief respite, McClellan prepared to renew his attack against Richmond. However, southern reinforcements arrived and under strong leadership of the Confederate generals, McClellan and his Union forces ultimately were blocked from attacking Richmond.

ARRIVAL BY WATER

There is one marina at Yorktown, Riverwalk Landing, which is usually very busy, and reservations are recommended. There are significant currents at this location. On the south side of the York River is the Wormley Creek Marina. There is a narrow channel to enter Wormley Creek starting with Green "1" WB." This mark is eight miles west from "R 14." The marina is to port as you enter the Creek. They can accommodate up to 50-foot vessels and there are a limited number of slips. This is a working marina with gas/diesel and lifts. Call ahead for a reservation.

The other choice is the York River Yacht Haven on the north side of the York River on Sarah Creek. This is nine miles west from Red "14." As you enter Sarah Creek look for Green "5" and follow the marks less than half a mile to Yacht Haven to port. To visit the historic Yorktown Battlefield site, you will need transportation over the Coleman Memorial Bridge.

OVERNIGHT

The **York River Yacht Haven** is a large full-service boatyard with many activities. Gas and diesel are available. The marina welcomes transients with 295 slips that can accommodate vessels up to 160 feet. Amenities include electricity, ships store, pool, pump-out, laun-

The Yorktown Victory Monument at Yorktown, Virginia

free shuttle that visits each town at 20-minute intervals. The best way to capture everything is to purchase admission tickets to all three sites. Tickets are available at any of the Historic towns.

York River Yacht Haven can arrange transportation to Yorktown. Yacht Haven also offers complimentary use of a vehicle for up to one hour. Uber is also available.

While in this area things to see include:

• **Yorktown Battlefield Visitor Center** including the **Moore House** where negotiations for Cornwallis' surrender were carried out.
Phone: 757-898-2410

• **Yorktown Victory Monument** Just across the street from the Hornsby House Inn stands a huge 84 ft. edifice overlooking the York River.

• **Waterman's Museum**
Phone: 757-887-2641
309 Water Street

Other sites nearby should be seen if time allows:

• **Busch Gardens**
Phone: 757-229-4386
1 Busch Gardens Blvd

• **Jamestown**

• **Williamsburg**

EATERIES

• **Riverwalk Restaurant** is at the center of the action. Seafood and steaks with a lovely river view.
Phone: 757-875-1522
323 Water Street A-I

dry, private showers, and picnic areas with grills. A 60-ton travel-lift is available. They have a lovely restaurant, the York River Oyster Company.

Phone: 804-642-2156
Email: yryh@suntexmarinas.com

SIGHTS

The Historic Triangle includes Yorktown, Williamsburg, and Jamestown. There is a

- **Yorktown Pub**–Nice pub with a full menu and water views.
  Phone: 757-886-9964
  540 Water Street

- **YROC Coastal Bar & Grill**–Located on the York River in the Yacht Haven Marina in Gloucester Point.
  Phone: 804-792-1511
  8109 Yacht Haven Road

The Yorktown area is one of the best on our odyssey of historic places to visit on the Chesapeake Bay. For American history buffs, this is ground zero. Here is located the first English colony at Jamestown in 1607 and the historic battlefield where the defeat of the British at Yorktown occurred. All were seminal events in our history. And nearby is the lovely, well-preserved, historic Williamsburg.

To enjoy this area, allow adequate time. We suggest three nights minimum. Yorktown is a walking town, and most sites can be seen on foot. And if you need a day to relax by the pool, York River Yacht Haven is the place to do it.

For those who may want to stay on land for part of this trip, there are several places to stay in Yorktown. Our favorite is:

- **Hornsby House Inn B&B is** in the center of Yorktown.
  Phone: 757-369-0020
  702 Main Street
  Enjoy.

NEXT DESTINATION: HAMPTON, VIRGINIA - 31 Miles

After a refreshing three days visiting the Historic Triangle, we depart from our home base at the York River Yacht Haven on Sarah Creek and travel 31 miles south to the city of Hampton, Virginia. We retrace our course to exit the York River and target Red "14" and turn to starboard.

As we head south, we are entering one of the most heavily traveled shipping areas on the east coast. The four cities around the Hampton Roads Waterway include Newport News and Hampton to starboard and Norfolk and Portsmouth to port as we enter the Waterway. To the east of Norfolk is Virginia Beach and to the west is Suffolk. To the south of Norfolk is the city of Chesapeake. Virginia Beach is the largest city in Virginia by area, with 497 square miles. Naval Base Norfolk is the largest naval base in the world.

Chapter 11
Hampton, Virginia
HISTORY

In 1607, Captain John Smith, the English explorer who originally explored many of our ports-of-call, came ashore at the site now known as Hampton, Virginia. In 1609, Colonial settlers built a wooden fort at the site of Fort Monroe. The fort accommodated 50 people and had seven cannons for defense. The city of Hampton was founded the following year.

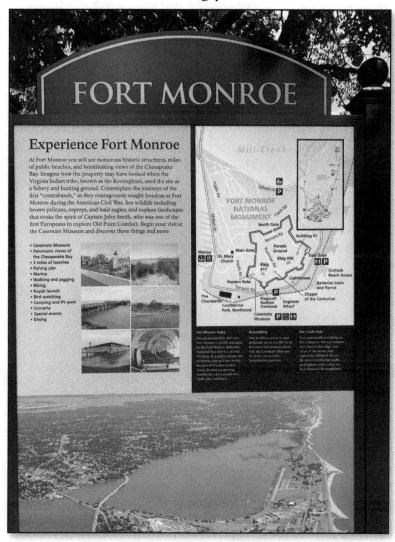

Fort Monroe, Virginia

Much of the history of Hampton revolves around Fort Monroe and the military. Fort Monroe was named after James Monroe, the fifth US president and last of the Founding Father Presidents. Construction was started in 1819 as a reaction to the War of 1812, where the British Navy ravaged the towns and cities on the Chesapeake Bay. A significant battle took place near Norfolk in June 1813. The British attacked a contingent of Americans by land and sea on Craney Island on the western side of the Elizabeth River. This Island was important because it was the last point of resistance to protect Norfolk where the *USS Constellation* was anchored. During the short engagement, the British were turned back; one of their few defeats during the War. In response, they decided to attack the poorly defended town of Hampton on June 25th. Under the command of the British were French troops who had been released from British prisons under the condition that they would fight in the War of 1812. After brief American resistance at Hampton, the French troops ran amuck and engaged in murder, rape, and pillage. Some American prisoners were shot. Even some British officers were appalled. A mere two months later the British would attack and burn Washington, D.C.

Fort Monroe was completed in 1836. Robert E. Lee of the Army CORPS of Engineers played a role in the completion of the Fort (recall he also oversaw the construction of Fort Carroll on the Patapsco River near Baltimore). Fort Monroe is surrounded by a moat and is the largest fort in the US. On its 63 acres there are 170 historic buildings. Fort Monroe is now preserved as the Fort Monroe National Monument and is open to the public.

Across the mouth of Hampton Roads another fort was built in this era, Fort Calhoun, named after John C. Calhoun, the Secretary of War at the time. The fort was later re-named after Civil War General John Wool. Cannons were placed in Fort Wool and Fort Monroe so that the entrance to Hampton Roads was protected from ship attacks. Again, the ubiquitous Robert E. Lee was involved in Fort Wool's construction. Presidents Andrew Jackson and John Tyler visited Fort Wool as a quiet respite after the death of their respective wives.

Fort Monroe played a significant role in the Civil War. Although in Virginia, a Confederate state, Fort Monroe remained in Union hands. In fact, the Fort became known as Freedom Fortress because over 10,000 fugitive slaves took refuge there during the four years of the War. As noted above, Union General George McClellan landed his army at Fort Monroe in preparation for the attack on Richmond.

POINT OF INTEREST

One of the most important naval battles in history took place in Hampton Roads within sight of Fort Monroe. On March 9, 1862, the two ironclad ships, *Monitor* (Union) and *Merrimac* (Confederate) battled it out for over four hours in the waters of Hampton Roads. Neither ship was sunk, and the result was inconclusive in spite of multiple cannonball strikes. This battle forever changed naval warfare with the conversion from wooden vessels, used since ancient times, to iron and steel ships.

As discussed in the section on Annapolis, President Abraham Lincoln visited Fort Monroe on February 2, 1865 to negotiate an end to the Civil War. The effort was unsuccessful.

After the end of the Civil War, the president of the Confederacy, Jefferson Davis, was captured and arrested in Georgia. He was imprisoned at Fort Monroe for two years in Casemate 92, now part of the museum tour.

During the two World Wars, defensive guns were upgraded at Fort Monroe and Fort Wool, but no action was seen.

At least 14 US presidents have visited Fort Monroe. One other prominent visitor spent the night at Fort Monroe on October 24, 1824. He was Marquis de Lafayette, the last surviv-

Casemate 92 at Fort Monroe, Virginia

ing Revolutionary War General, who visited the United States for 13 months during 1824. He was invited by President Monroe to tour the expanding new country and to remind the population of the sacrifices made by the Revolutionary War generation.

ARRIVAL BY WATER

As you proceed south along the western shore you will see Thimble Shoal Light that is 55 feet in height. There are many naval and commercial craft in this busy port; keep your distance. You will proceed to the mile-wide entrance to Hampton Roads and you can take a look to port and see the 4-5 mile length of Naval Base Norfolk. We chose to overnight close to Old Point Comfort on the Hampton River.

On the south side entrance from the Bay into the Hampton Roads is Fort Wool on Rip Raps Island. On the north side of the river entrance at Old Point Comfort, is Fort Monroe. As you pass Old Point Comfort one can see the nine-story Chamberlain Hotel, where I once stayed as a youngster with my family. It is now a senior living center.

Fort Monroe is surrounded by a moat and is located near the old hotel. The 54-foot, Old Point Comfort Lighthouse was built on the grounds of Fort Monroe in 1802 and is easily seen as you approach. As you round Old Point Comfort give wide latitude to Red "2" just outside the rocky abutments surrounding the concrete entrance to the underwater Hampton Roads tunnel.

The opposite opening of the tunnel is on the south side of Hampton Roads adjacent to Fort Wool.

Old Point Comfort Lighthouse on the grounds of Fort Monroe

At some point during your trip, we recommend that you take a short cruise southward past the enormous yards of Naval Base Norfolk and see the vast number of ships. It is very impressive. We spent about an hour cruising down the Elizabeth River and saw three aircraft carriers, several cruisers, destroyers, and many support ships. It is impressive. This area is a restricted area, meaning that you will be observed as you cruise through and be subject to stop and search. Small patrol boats may track you and document your speed, so do not exceed five knots. If the weather is good and you have the time, you may want to take this short tour before you tie up for the night on the Hampton River, as we did.

Incidentally, Mile Mark 0 (Red Buoy "36"), about four miles south of Naval Base Norfolk, is the northern starting point of the 1,000-mile Intracoastal Waterway. The ICW winds to Florida along an inland course protected from the ocean. The ICW terminates in Miami.

OVERNIGHT

• **Bluewater Yachting Center** is on the west side of the Hampton River shortly beyond Green "13" to port. They offer floating docks for boats and yachts up to 200 ft. This is a very nice marina with 200 slips. Amenities include a swimming pool & guest area, group pavilion, picnic & grill area, Wi-Fi, laundry, showers, high-speed fuel pumps, taxi service, a service yard, haulout basin, Ship's Store,

and the Surfrider Restaurant. The marina is close to the many attractions in Hampton.
Waypoint: 37° 01.28 N / 76° 20.589 W
Phone: 757-723-6774

We elected to stay at the Bluewater Yachting Center for two nights.

• Other choices are the **Old Point Comfort Marina**, which is a full-service marina offering accommodations for more than 300 boats up to 50 ft. in length. Amenities include gas, diesel, pump-out services, and a Ship's Store. The Deadrise Restaurant is a casual café offering salads, sandwiches, and light fare. Open for lunch and dinner, but days and hours vary by the season. It is a short walk to Fort Monroe.
Phone: 757-788-4308

SIGHTS

• **Fort Monroe**–Spend half a day exploring the largest military fort in the US. The Fort is now operated by the National Park Service. Be sure to visit the Casemate 92 inside the Fort where Confederate President Jefferson Davis was imprisoned after the end of the Civil War. Unfortunately, there is no longer a ferry boat trip available to Fort Wool-it is now a designated bird sanctuary.

• **Virginia Air and Space Museum** A must-see for the whole family. It is filled with great exhibits of military airplanes, rocket models, and actual space capsules. Spend at least half a day here.
Phone: 757-727-0900
600 Settlers Landing Road

• **Miss Hampton II Harbor Cruises** This 3-hour cruise around Hampton Roads includes a trip past Naval Base

Naval Base, Norfolk, Virginia

A rare double rainbow from the dock of the Bluewater Yachting Center, Hampton, Virginia

Norfolk. I usually do not recommend local cruise trips since you are arriving by boat. But if you do not sail past the navy yard yourself, take the Miss Hampton II cruise. Lunch is available aboard.
Phone: 757-722-9102
710 Settlers Landing Road

• **Hampton Indoor Coliseum**–Check to see what shows are available when you visit Hampton.
Phone: 757-838-4203
1000 Coliseum Drive

If you are spending a few days you should visit other sights in the area. You can travel to these Norfolk sites by cab or Uber. We recommend:

• **Naval Station Norfolk Tour** this guided land tour takes you around the base to see some 70 ships and 130 aircraft. Reservations are required.
Phone: 757-444-7955
9079 Hampton Blvd

• **Nauticus Museum** including a tour of the World War II Battleship the *USS Wisconsin*. Do not miss exploring this magnificent ship.
Phone: 757-664-1000
One Waterside Drive

• **General Douglas MacArthur Memorial**–The memorial consists of a museum, archive and research center, education center, theater, welcome center, and a gift shop. A visit to the Memorial will allow you to explore the life of one of America's greatest and most complex military leaders. Admission is FREE.
Phone: 757-441-2965
198 Bank Street

We suggest two or three nights in Hampton to see all the sights.

EATERIES

• **Park Lane Tavern** in Peninsula Town Center. European atmosphere, lovely facility. You will need to take an Uber.
Phone: 757-838-2748
4200 Kilgore Avenue

• **Surf Rider Restaurant** is located at the Bluewater Yachting Center. American cuisine with great seafood.
Phone: 757-723-9366
1 Marina Road

• **The Barking Dog**–Great sandwiches, dogs, and burgers.
Phone: 757-325-8352
4330 Kecoughtan Road

• **Old Hampton Seafood Kitchen** located in Downtown Hampton, Virginia claims

The Virginia Air & Space Center at Hampton, Virginia

Some displays at the Virginia Air & Space Center at Hampton, Virginia

to have the best fried seafood and seafood sandwiches in town.

Phone: 757-723-5777
124 S. Annistead Road

NEXT DESTINATION: CAPE CHARLES, VIRGINIA - 24 Miles

Cape Charles, Virginia is about 24 miles from Hampton across the southern Bay. This is an historic town with a modern, new development known as the Oyster Farm at Kings Creek Marina, which includes a golf course and a large, new marina.

The short 24-mile cruise to Cape Charles offers a day to sleep in late (i.e. an 8:00 a.m. departure from Hampton). With decent weather, you should tie up at Cape Charles by 11:00 a.m. This will allow time to wander around and explore this charming and historic town.

Chapter 12
Cape Charles, Virginia
HISTORY

Cape Charles is one of the earliest planned communities in the US. In 1883, William Scott, a railroad man from Erie, PA, purchased 2,500 acres of land and deeded part of it to the New York, Philadelphia, and Norfolk Railroad. Scott's vision was to allow freight and passengers to connect from the DelMarVa peninsula to Norfolk and Hampton. The railroad spur from Pocomoke City, Maryland to Cape Charles, Virginia was completed in 1884. That same year the natural harbor was dredged, and steamboats began transporting freight and passengers from Cape Charles to Norfolk. Currently, the town has a year-round population of about 1,000.

An old buoy and little girl at the front entrance of the Shanty Restaurant in Cape Charles, Virginia

Cape Charles consisted of 136 acres and was incorporated in 1886. It was laid out as a square grid, 7 x 7 blocks. The roads running east/west are named after famous Virginia statesmen and are called 'Avenue' and the roads running north/south are named after fruits and called 'Street.' The town prospered with railroad and steamboat connections. Train service arrived daily from New York City. Streets were paved, new homes went up and the town grew rapidly. Electricity, telephones, and water and sewer made Cape Charles the most cosmopolitan city on the DelMarVa peninsula.

An old passenger train car at Cape Charles, Virginia

eter underwater crater was made, with no surface remnants visible today. It is known as the Chesapeake Bay Impact Crater.

Football fans may remember a defensive back for the Baltimore Colts, Johnny Sample. He was from Cape Charles.

ARRIVAL BY WATER

Departure from Hampton is a reversal of your entrance. Remember to keep a good distance from all naval and commercial craft through this busy area and pay attention to Channel 16, as always. Head past Old Point Comfort and leave the Thimble Shoal Light tower (55 feet) to starboard, then take a northeast course of about 50 degrees toward Flashing Red Buoy "20" marking the eastern margin of the York Spit Channel.

While we cruised across the Bay toward Cape Charles, we could see the Chesapeake Bay Bridge Tunnel off in the distance to starboard. Another surprising sight was two blue-hulled fishing boats trolling the waters off Cape Charles. They were the menhaden vessels we had seen docked in Reedville, VA!

As you approach Cape Charles, look for a Green Can "1 CC." It is very small — could not be taller than two feet in height and is easily missed. Near this green can, look to starboard and you will see the collapsed ruins of the Old Plantation Light. You will then spot Red Can "2," followed by Red "4," Red "6," and Red "8." There is a range light as you follow in these Red Marks, but its use is not necessary in daylight. As you pass Red "8" turn to starboard into the wide City Harbor. There is a large and busy stone/concrete plant to starboard as you enter the Harbor. The City and Cape Charles

Gradually, steamboat services around the Bay would wind down, but ferry boat car service from Cape Charles to Norfolk continued until 1964 when the Chesapeake Bay Bridge Tunnel opened. A railroad freight barge remained in operation from Cape Charles until 2018.

Today, Cape Charles has evolved into a tourist destination with lovely beaches, golf courses, shops, and restaurants. One mile north of the old town of Cape Charles is the newly developed community, the Oyster Farm at King's Creek with a large marina, rental properties and restaurants. By car, the drive from Norfolk to this resort is only an hour over the Bridge-Tunnel.

POINT OF INTEREST.

One interesting historical footnote is worth mentioning. About 35 million years ago in the Eocene Era, a bolide (meteor) struck a point where Cape Charles is located. A 25-mile diam-

The lovely beach at Cape Charles, Virginia

We took the 10-minute walk to the town of Cape Charles from the marina. It is a charming little city with a busy main street, Mason Avenue. We walked along this street and shopped and then had lunch at Kelley's Gingernut Pub.

The parking arrangement is atypical in that all cars must back into parking places at a 45-degree angle. Out-of-towners struggle with this. It is not clear why this is the requirement.

Also, of note is the considerable number of golf carts — it seems everyone has one.

Golf carts can be rented at:

- **CC Ryder Rentals**
  Phone: 757-678-3239
  415 Mason Avenue

Bicycles are also extremely popular. We walked to the rectangular central open-air park with a large fountain. The wide streets have many large homes with a mix of smaller ones. All appear to be well kept and there is a considerable rebuilding of old knockdowns. As you walk closer to the beach the homes get larger. Houses across the street from the beach — there are no homes directly on the beach- are rather large with wonderful water views. A high sand dune, perhaps 15 ft above sea level, runs along the whole length of the beach providing considerable protection from flooding and storm surges. The beach itself is perhaps 100 yards in width and is notable for its fine, white sand. During our visit, there was little wave action, so young children could walk out some distance without getting knocked down. This is a great spot for photos of sunsets.

Town Harbor & Marina are to port. The marina office can be identified by a green roof.

OVERNIGHT

- **Cape Charles Harbor**–We stayed at the city-owned Cape Charles Harbor & Marina. They can accommodate commercial and recreational vessels in a protective basin. They offer 95 slips, 4 T-heads ranging from 60 to 120 feet, and 1,200 feet of dock space. Fuel, internet, shore power, and showers are available.
  Phone: 757-331-2357
  Email: dockmaster@ccyachtcenter.com

Cape Charles is a unique town with many amenities. We stayed two nights. Other sights:

- **Cape Charles Museum**–It is only open on Saturdays.
  Phone: 757-331-1008
  814 Randolph Avenue

- **Palace Theater**–The theatre features a full season of arts entertainment, engaging performing artists of local and international renown.
  Phone: 757-331-2787
  305 Mason Avenue

- **Oyster Farm at King's Creek** a one-mile walk—check out the charming, colorful homes, new marina, pool, and nice restaurant. The marina is huge with the main pier extending out 200 yards.
  Phone: 757-331-8660
  500 Marina Village Circle

- **Bay Creek Resort and Club**–Enjoy 27 holes of Palmer and Nicklaus golf just two miles from Cape Charles.
  Phone: 757-331-8600
  3335 Stone Road

EATERIES

- **The Shanty** at our dock offers great seafood
  Phone: 757-695-3853
  33 Marina Road

- **Kelly's Gingernut Pub**–Irish fare with generous portions.
  Phone: 757-331-3222
  133 Mason Avenue

- **Seafood Eatery at Oyster Farm Marina** is a one-mile walk from town. Also, visit the C-Pier Dock Bar at the end of the long pier.
  Phone: 757-331-8660
  500 Marina Village Circle

- **Cape Charles Brewing Company**–For beer lovers including a raw bar with a great menu.
  Phone: 757-695-3909
  2198 Stone Road

- **Hook @ Harvey** is a Gourmet Bistro on the waterfront. Reservations are recommended. It is a short walk from the marina. This restaurant is said to have the best food in town.
  Phone: 757-331-2275
  1011 Bay Shore Road

NEXT DESTINATION: ONANCOCK, VIRGINIA - 34 Miles

Onancock, pronounced with the emphasis on "NAN" is a small town of 1,200 residents located five miles in from the Chesapeake Bay at the origin of the Onancock Creek (Note: do not confuse this Creek with Occohannock Creek which is about 11 miles south of Onancock Creek).

Chapter 13
Onancock, Virginia
HISTORY

Before Europeans showed up, Onancock was inhabited by local Indian tribes. The name is of Indian derivation and means "a foggy place." The town was initially known as Port Scarborough, but in 1680 the Virginia House of Burgesses renamed the town Onancock and chartered it as an official port of entry. It became an important destination for commercial sailing vessels and later steam ships carrying farm produce and other goods.

During the American Revolution, a local militia barracks was established in Onancock. The British were proficient at harassing and attacking ports and villages throughout the Chesapeake. This continued even after the surrender of General Cornwallis at Yorktown in October 1781. After all, the War had not yet officially ended. The State of Maryland decided to take corrective action. Commodore Zedechiah Whaley of the Maryland State Navy was ordered to clear the British from Bay waters. He took a small flotilla of four armed barges that used oars and sail power. Whaley spotted a larger force of British barges in Tangier Sound and realized that he needed more men. He sailed into Onancock seeking assistance. With the help of the local militia under Lt. Col. John Cropper, 25 additional men went to aid Commodore Whaley. On November 30, 1782, more than a year after the surrender of Cornwallis, The Battle of the Barges took place in Kedges Strait just north of Smith Island. The Americans were outgunned and most of the sailors and three barges escaped. The British captured some of the sailors and Commodore Whaley was killed in action.

Ironically, the Battle of the Barges occurred on the same day the Treaty of Peace was drafted. The treaty ended the hostilities between the US and Great Britain. This small battle was the last naval action of the Revolution. The final Treaty of Paris was not signed, ratified, and exchanged until May 12, 1784. The Americans signed the Treaty in Annapolis at the Maryland State House.

ARRIVAL BY WATER

Departing from Cape Charles, retrace your entrance and follow the marks south to Green Buoy "1 CC" then north at 340 degrees to Red Nun "36A." A course of 22 degrees will carry you north, parallel to the coast toward Tangier Sound. Proceed 12 miles north to Red Nun "42A," passing Red Nun "38A," and Red Nun "40A." Adjust course to 12 degrees for 4.5 miles past the unnamed 31-foot tower, then adjust to course 38 degrees, for 5.7 miles to Red Nun "54A." Modify the course to 32 degrees for 6.7 miles to a 15-foot Red "2." Turn to starboard at 108 degrees for 2.5 miles to a 15-foot Green "1" This marks the entrance to Onancock Creek. Follow the daymarks carefully; the Creek meanders left and right. As the Creek narrows close to the headwaters (about five miles from Green "1Y"), you will see the Onancock Wharf and Mallards Restaurant. When the Wharf is in sight call them on Ch. 16 for docking instructions. There is nowhere else to tie up for your visit. The staff there is extremely helpful and pleasant.

OVERNIGHT

As noted, we tied up for one night at the Onancock Wharf. They have nice, clean showers, ice, diesel, and gasoline. There are 17 slips, mostly for 35-40-foot boats. The largest spot for our 61-foot vessel was at the bulkhead. The staff supplied us with an excellent walking map of the town. Kayaks and bicycles are available for rent. At the Wharf, the staff introduced us to a unique service we had never seen offered elsewhere. They gave us a list of about 15 local residents who were willing to take transient boaters by car to a local shopping center for gro-

ceries or supplies. We did not need this service but greatly appreciated the offer.

SIGHTS

Once we cleaned up, we took a short walk to the center of this charming town. There are many shops, restaurants, art galleries, and one hotel, The Charlotte. On recommendation of a local shopkeeper, we had dinner at The Charlotte Hotel and enjoyed an excellent meal.

- If you have time, visit the **Ker Place Historic House Museum** near the center of town. It is the finest example of Federal architecture on the Eastern Shore of Virginia and has lovely grounds and a Colonial herb garden. Admission is by donation.
  Phone: 757-787-8012
  69 Market Street

EATERIES

- **The Charlotte Hotel**–The restaurant in this charming hotel is excellent.
  Phone: 757-787-7400
  7 North Street

- **Mallards**–With two full bars, one inside and one on their spacious deck.
  Phone: 757-787-8558
  2 Market Street

- **Bizzotto's Gallery Caffé**–The menu features international cuisine and local delicacies such as crab cakes and soft crabs in season.
  Phone: 757-787-3103
  41 Market Street

- **Blarney Stone Pub**
  Phone: 757-302-0300
  10 North Street

- **Janet's Café Coffee**–Comfort food, healthy options, a quick bite, and Vegetarian options
  Phone: 757-787-9495
  49 King Street

The view from the Onancock City Wharf

NEXT DESTINATION: CRISFIELD, MARYLAND - 24 Miles

Just west of Crisfield are two historic Islands: Tangier Island, about 12 miles southwest, and Smith Island, about 10 miles due west. We debated whether or not to visit each Island for a night on our boat, but decided to tie up in Crisfield, Maryland, and use that as our base to make day-trips to each island via daily launches. Departing from Onancock, retrace your course and proceed to Green "1." Then turn north at a course of 318 degrees for six miles toward Tangier Sound Light which is 45 feet in height. Then proceed at 10 degrees north (or 28 degrees if your starting point is Tangier Sound Light) to Green "5." Then 3.3 miles at course 19 degrees to Red Buoy "6" which marks the Maryland-Virginia line. Then 3.3 miles at 34 degrees to Green Can "Cl." Enter Crisfield Harbor keeping to starboard Red "2," Red "4," and Red "8." Just beyond Red "10," look to starboard next for the narrow channel that leads into Somers Cove. The channel starts at the base of the tall condo and is difficult to see until you are nearly upon it. Proceed into the Channel and Somers Cove Marina is straight ahead at the back of the harbor to port.

Chapter 14
Crisfield, Maryland

With Day Trips to Tangier and Smith Islands
HISTORY

We will review the history of Crisfield and then each island separately along with our journeys to each.

Crisfield, Maryland. The town was founded in 1663 by Benjamin Summers. The original Indian name of Annemssex was changed to Somers Cove. As seafood became more popular, a local attorney, John W. Crisfield, arranged to have a railroad spur built to Somers Cove around 1866. He was part owner of the Eastern Shore Railroad; an arrangement that permitted large shipments of oysters around the eastern seaboard. In honor of the man who put the town on the map, the name was changed to Crisfield in 1872. Crisfield was elected to the US House of Representatives in 1847 and became a friend of Abraham Lincoln.

The town became known as the Oyster Capital of the World and by 1904 Crisfield was the second-largest city in Maryland (after Baltimore) with over 25,000 residents. Eventually, after years of over-harvesting oysters, Crisfield's seafood industry evolved into crabbing and the town became the Crab Capital of the World. More enlightened ideas prevailed, and it is now known as the Seafood Capital of the US (or is it the World?).

A popular Maryland governor, J. Millard Tawes, who served from 1959-1967, was from Crisfield. Today, Crisfield is connected by boat to Smith and Tangier Islands for their supplies, food, visitors,

mail, and delivering children to and from schools.

Crisfield is known for its annual National Hard Crab Derby celebrated each Labor Day weekend. Activities include hard crab races, carnivals, children's rides, music, boat docking contests, entertainment including the Miss Crustacean Beauty Contest, and of course, many crabs in various forms for human consumption.

ARRIVAL BY WATER

To cruise from Onancock to Crisfield, continue north into Tangier Sound (leave Pocomoke Sound to starboard). See detailed notes above under NEXT DESTINATION at the end of Chapter 13.

Colorful crab pot floats on Tangier Island

As you approach Crisfield from the Bay, the most prominent landmark from afar is the 375-foot wind turbine located in the center of Crisfield. It is used to supply electricity to the water treatment plant for the city. It began operating in February 2017 after two years of construction. I know of no other wind turbine that is located in the center of a town.

OVERNIGHT

- We elected to tie up at **Somers Cove Marina** at Crisfield and stayed for two nights. This is a state-owned pet-friendly marina with 100 transient slips up to 150 feet. Amenities include 30, 50, and 100-amp electric, swimming pool, a playground, air-conditioned bath houses, laundry facilities, picnic tables & barbecue grills, horseshoe pits, Wi-Fi hot spots, pump-out stations, and a Ship's Store.
Phone: 410-968-0925
Email:
dockmaster@SomersCoveMarina.com

There is a good marine store a few blocks from the Marina; Goldsborough Marine. Here is the spot to stock up on supplies. It is easy to find; it is just under the town water tower.

We spent about half a day exploring Crisfield, visiting Goldsborough Marine store, and checking out the City Dock where boats depart daily for Smith Island (45-minute trip) and Tangier Island (one-hour trip). On separate days we visited each of the Islands.

SIGHTS

Crisfield is an old waterman's town and small enough to walk to most places. Everything is oriented toward seafood, of course. Worth a visit is:

The wind turbine at Crisfield, Maryland

• **J. Millard Tawes Historical Museum**–Explore interpretive exhibits about Crisfield's distinctive maritime past, including natural history, the crab, oyster industries, shipbuilding, decoys, and much more.
Phone: 410-968-2501
3 9th Street

EATERIES

• **The Waterman's Inn**–American cuisine offering lots of seafood with excellent menu.
Phone: 410-968-2119
901 W. Main Street

• **Café Milano**–Great Italian dishes and excellent pizza. About a mile walk from the marina but they will deliver.
Phone: 410-968-1082
103 N 4th Street

• **Captain Tyler's Crab House**-Traditional casual crab house. Tyler's is within walking distance of the marina.
Phone: 410-968-1131
923 Spruce Street

• **Smith Island Baking Company**–Check their website for their spectacular cakes, baked goods, and ice cream. A one-mile walk.
Phone: 410-968-1131
45 W. Chesapeake Avenue

• **Red Shell Shanty Restaurant**–Sandwich shop three blocks from the marina.
Phone: 443-614-2397
715 Broadway

• **Tangier Island, Virginia**–Like most tidewater areas of the Chesapeake Bay, American Indians were the earliest occupants of Tangier Island. In 1608, Captain John Smith visited this island as he seemed to do with many shores of the Bay. Rumor states that Captain Smith had sailed the world and his favorite port was

Tangier, Morocco. The long white beaches of this primitive bay island reminded him of Tangier and the name stuck. Ownership of the island passed through many English inhabitants of Virginia.

POINT OF INTEREST

The island played a strange role in the War of 1812. Our old friend, Admiral George Cockburn, used Tangier Island as a port and staging area for his naval attacks on Washington, Baltimore, and other ports of his choosing. On the Island, the British built Fort Albion (the Latin term for England) with as many as 1,200 British troops stationed there. It was built on the southernmost point on the Island and had a parade ground, housing for troops and officers, and a hospital. Before the British troops attacked Baltimore, a local Parson, Joshua Thomas, was asked to give the troops a blessing on the beach at a religious service. He warned the British that what they were about to do was wrong and he predicted they would not succeed. He was correct. No evidence of Fort Albion remains.

In May 1886, all the inhabitants of Tangier Island were evacuated because of a lethal epidemic, most likely cholera. The quarantine lasted for 13 months. Only about half the residents returned to their homes on the Island. Our casual conversations with locals suggested there have been no cases of Covid on Tangier Island as of August 2020.

Today, the inhabitants occupy themselves as watermen, catching all the Bay will yield. In the spring and summer, crabs are the catch. In the fall and winter, oysters bring in the revenue. Fishing goes on year around. About 600 people reside on Tangier Island. The English descendants on the Island trace their ancestors back to the area of Cornwall, England and it is said the English dialect spoken here resembles that of Cornwall residents. You can best discern the dialect if you are able to listen to the Islanders speak to each other. When they speak to mainland folks, they seem to modify their dialect.

The flag displayed on the Island has the logo from Cornwall in its upper left quadrant, a black field with a white cross.

We took the "mail boat" to Tangier Island. The round-trip cost was $27 per person. We boarded at the City Dock in Crisfield. The 60-foot vessel departed at 12:30 p.m. and the one-hour trip was pleasant on a lovely, windless August day. The private vessel was named *Courtney Thomas*. It is not exclusively a "mail boat" since it also carries residents of Tangier Island, visitors, groceries, UPS and FedEx boxes, lumber, batteries, car parts, and whatever

A brief history about Fort Albion on Tangier Island, Virginia

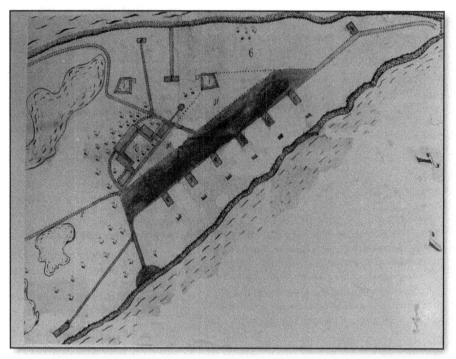

A sketch of the British Fort Albion, which during the War of 1812 was located on the southern tip of Tangier Island, Virginia.

Colorful Tangier Island crab pots

supplies are needed on the Island. As we approached the Island there were many shanties along the waterway, with dozens of multi-colored crab pots (traps) stacked up on the sagging piers. When the *Courtney Thomas* arrived at the Island dock, numerous people were waiting. Many had their golf carts ready to pick up supplies.

We got off the boat and found within one block a cute little eating establishment, Fisherman's Corner Restaurant. The Tangier Vegetable Crab Soup was delicious and highly recommended. We then took a guided tour by Miss Claudia in her golf cart. We saw several restaurants, two churches, two health clinics, a few cute shops, and many homes. We drove past the one airport on the Island that was used by small aircraft. We saw the one school. The Island is flat and marshy.

With each hurricane or heavy storm, the Island gets flooded and more of its real estate is washed into the Bay. We observed several homes with one or two inches of water in their front and back yards. No need to cut the lawn! Most homes are built up on cinder blocks. We also observed many homes that were deserted and collapsing. When folks decided to leave, they apparently walked away from their homes and no one claimed them.

Tidal flooding on Tangier Island, Virginia

Smith Island is about 10 miles north of Tangier Island and is slightly larger than its southern neighbor. Smith Island is in Maryland, although some marshy, southern extensions of the Island fall within the boundary of Virginia. About 270 people reside here and they too, like Tangier Island, trace their lineage back to Cornwall, England. The Smith Island flag is a near replica of the one from Tangier Island with the Cornwall logo in its top left quadrant.

The residents rely on the Bay to make a living as watermen, much like the residents of Tangier. When visiting, be sure to sample the famous, multi-layered Smith Island Cake. In 2009, it was designated as the official Dessert of the State of Maryland.

There is no airport on Smith Island. But there are three "towns" on the Island. The main town is Ewell where the commuter vessels dock and depart. Toward the south is Rhodes Point, little more than a cluster of homes. To the southeast is the

When we later walked around part of the island, I looked for some remnant of Fort Albion on the southern point of the island. There was nothing left of the British Fort, only flat green marshland and white beaches. The locals confirmed our finding.

The vessel *Sharon Kay 111* departed Tangier Island at 4:00 p.m. and returned us to Crisfield.

- **Smith Island, Maryland**–Smith Island was apparently named after an early landowner named Henry Smith. It was once known as the "Russell Isles." A private daily boat to Smith Island departs from the City Dock at Crisfield at 12:30 p.m. (the same time as the boat to Tangier Island). That same commuter vessel leaves Smith Island at 4:00 p.m. and takes passengers back to Crisfield. The roundtrip fee was $25 per person.

town of Tylertown that requires a boat to visit. We did not visit Tylertown. Between the towns, there are large swaths of swamps and grasses. There are many deserted, collapsing homes and former businesses. Covid has not helped the tourist industry here.

We had lunch near the Ewell city dock. The soft crab sandwich was mediocre; a great surprise for an Island full of crabs and experts at preparing the bounty of the Bay.

I learned there is one marina for transient boats on Smith Island. It is owned by Capt. Parks, a charming gentleman who, despite being in his eighties, still scampers around and helps with docking. Capt. Parks has several slips for 45-foot boats and a T-head dock of about 50 feet. There is electric for each slip. To check for slip availability, one should call Capt. Parks in advance. He often does not answer the phone, so just tie up and he will find you and your boat in the evening.

My wife and I had visited Smith Island in 1985 and we spent one night on our sailboat at a rundown dock in Ewell. We had dinner at Mrs. Kitching's home. She was a well-known cook on the island and has a famous cookbook credited to her. We had an excellent meal, and she was a gracious host. On this second trip, we learned that she had passed away and her house had been knocked down for a new home that so far consisted only of a few rows of cinder blocks. We noted on this visit that there were more homes on the Island and many golf carts. There were no golf carts in 1985.

I recall one humorous episode which occurred during our 1985 visit. After our wonderful repast at Mrs. Kitchings, we retired to our 30-foot Bristol sailboat. We were fast asleep in the "V" berth, when suddenly, at about 4:00 a.m., we were startled and aroused by an explosion-like noise of undetermined cause. I was slightly delirious, but quickly opened the forward hatch above us and was instantly exposed to an extraordinarily bright light which seemed to fill the sky. Was this the end of the world? After we regained our senses, we came to recognize that this was a simultaneous gathering of the watermen at the adjacent dock. They all started their engines together and had illuminated the dock with all the bright lights. As our pulses slowed, we watched them motor out into the Bay to begin the labor of watermen.

During the 2020 visit I spoke to a young lady at a local gift shop. She knew the author, Tom Horton, who wrote "An Island out of Time: A Memoir of Smith Island in the Chesapeake." Tom lived in the town of Tylertown for two years with his family. His book is excellent and reveals the good, the bad, and the ugly about Smith Island.

Golf carts and bicycles are for rent on the Island. We chose to get a golf cart for one hour, which gives plenty of time to see most of the sites. The other good reason to rent a golf cart is that you can move quickly enough to avoid the bugs. Bicycles lack that advantage. We visited the one church, the charming tiny Post Office, Rhodes Point, and a gift shop.

Although these two Islands are quiet with few sights to see, I recommend a day trip to each for the experience. The residents of both Islands are friendly and very gracious. There are few places like this remaining in the United States. And they may not last forever.

NEXT DESTINATION: CAMBRIDGE, MARYLAND - 68 Miles

Departing from Crisfield, retrace your arrival course. Leave the 37-foot Janes Island Light to starboard and proceed to nearby Red Buoy "8." From here take a course of 29 degrees for 2 miles to Green Buoy "9." Turn to port on a course of 319 degrees for five miles to Green Can "5." Set a course for 295 degrees for five miles to Holland Island Bar, a 37-foot light. You will leave Solomons

Lump Light, with its 47-foot light to port as you progress through Kedges Straits. This light has an unusual configuration: the rectangular housing for the light rests on the side of the round base which gives it a distinctive appearance. This Strait is narrow between the north tip of Smith Island and the south tip of South Marsh Island (uninhabited).

POINT OF INTEREST

If you recall it was in the Kedges Straits near the Solomons Lump Light, where the Battle of the Barges took place. This small battle was the last naval engagement of the American Revolution (see notes under Onancock History).

From Holland Island Bar proceed north on a course of 338 degrees for 13 miles to the 63-foot Hooper Island Light. Continue at 346 degrees past Red Buoy "74" onto Red Buoy "76" (6.5 miles). Modify course to 352 degrees for 11 miles to Red Nun "2." From here, bear to starboard toward the Choptank River on a course of 32 degrees for five miles. The next mark is Green Can "5." Be sure to leave this can well to port; beyond it are the shallows of the partially submerged Sharps Island. Modify your course slightly to 30 degrees for two miles to Green Buoy "7." Turn more to starboard at 78 degrees for 1.5 miles to Red Buoy "10." Then more to starboard on a course of 97 degrees. After 5.7 miles you will encounter the 35-foot old Choptank River Light. From here, if you proceed north at 18 degrees, a short 2.3 miles, you will arrive at the charming town of Oxford, Maryland, which we will visit after we depart from Cambridge. From the old Choptank River Light, follow the marks 7.3 miles to Green Can "25" then to starboard into Cambridge, just before the Rt. 50 bridge.

To gain entrance to either the Municipal Marina or the Cambridge Yacht Club, look for the set of private green/red small floating buoys that are directed toward the rebuilt replica of the Choptank River Screw-Pile Lighthouse at the Municipal Marina. Run parallel to the Rt 50 bridge. As you get close to the floating dock, look to port to see what appears to be the opening in a maze. This is the entrance to the protected harbor. As you enter, the maze will direct you to port to an open fairway. Once in the fairway, to port is the Municipal Marina; to starboard is the Cambridge Yacht Club.

Solomons Lump Light in Kedges Straits, the site of the Battle of the Barges. This was the last naval engagement of the American Revolution.

Chapter 15
Cambridge, Maryland
HISTORY

Cambridge, Maryland was settled by English colonists in 1684. The area had been occupied by the Choptank Indians. It became a farming area and the town served as an early trading center. The city was named after Cambridge, England and was incorporated in 1793.

After the American Revolution, the British were in a snit and refused to import tobacco from Cambridge. The residents became even more anti-British. During the Civil War Era, the town of Cambridge was a stop for the Underground Railroad that aided slaves who were escaping to the North. Harriett Tubman was from Cambridge. She was active in the Underground movement. Be sure to visit the Tubman Museum dedicated to her.

The heavily wooded area around Cambridge was conducive to boat building. Thus, Cambridge became a center for building many fishing and crabbing boats for Bay watermen.

During the World Wars, Cambridge was active in canning tomatoes, sweet potatoes, and oysters for the Army. The Phillips Packing Company received government contracts and, at one time, employed as many as 10,000 people. The economic boom did not last and by 1960 the Packing Company was closed. Social unrest followed and Cambridge was a site of civil disturbances when local African Americans became active in the Civil Rights Movement.

In 2002, the Hyatt Regency Chesapeake Bay Resort opened with a 400-room hotel, a mar- ina, a golf course, and a spa. This was a significant employment stimulant to the community.

Tourism is now a large component of economic life in Cambridge. About 12,300 people reside in Cambridge.

ARRIVAL BY WATER

When arriving at the city of Cambridge you will bear to starboard before reaching the Rt. 50, Cambridge River Bridge. If you elect to pass under the bridge and proceed to the Hyatt Regency Hotel Marina (reservations are recommended), the Bridge has a vertical clearance of 50 feet.

We elected to stay "in town" so we bore to starboard at Green Can "25" before the Bridge and followed the private channel marks via the Choptank River. We turned to starboard to enter the Cambridge Municipal Yacht Basin and docked at the Cambridge Yacht Club on a "T" head dock along the starboard side of the fairway.

OVERNIGHT

The Cambridge Municipal Yacht Basin is directly on the Choptank River but is well protected with a sea wall. They have

A replica of the Choptank Screw-Pile Lighthouse now located at the Cambridge City Dock.

to downtown as the crow flies, it is more like four miles by road; so a cab or Uber is appropriate to visit the city.

• **The Cambridge Yacht Club** is very charming with the best water views in town. The Yacht Club has deep water slips with floating docks for boats of all sizes and cruisers are welcome. Transient slips with water and electricity are available at the yacht club. Fuel service is available at the adjacent Cambridge Municipal Marina. Amenities include showers, ice, pumpout, Wi-Fi, and dockside gazebo dining in season for members and guests. The yacht club is pet friendly with a dog park and is walking distance to shopping, restaurants, and more.

Phone: 410-228-2141

The center of town is about 10 blocks from the Yacht Club. Walk up High Street where there are beautiful large homes on either side of the street. Some of the homes are historically significant. The center of town has a smart courthouse, a library, an impressive church, and many eateries and shops. We visited the Harriett Tubman Museum, but it was closed.

SIGHTS

• **Harriet Tubman Museum**–Known as the "Moses" of her people, Harriet Ross Tubman, an African American woman of great moral courage, has nobly earned her

floating docks, over 240 slips, gas, diesel, and showers. The marina is within a short walk of all the activities of downtown.

The Hyatt Regency Chesapeake Resort has a fine marina. Overnighters at the marina have use of all the Hotel amenities, including the pool and golf course. There is an excellent restaurant in the hotel, The Blue Point Provision Company. The only disadvantage of staying at the hotel marina is that you miss the excitement of the activities in downtown Cambridge. Even though the hotel is less than two miles

The Spocott Windmill dating from circa 1850

• Richardson Maritime Museum–Named for a local boat builder. Dedicated to the craftsmen and culture of Eastern Shore boat building. The museum holds an exquisite collection of Chesapeake Bay ship models and artifacts bringing alive the local maritime heritage.
Phone: 410-221-1871
401 High Street

• Annie Oakley House–In 1912, this home was designed by and built for Wild West Sharpshooter Annie Oakley when she and her husband Frank Butler retired to Cambridge. This house is now a private residence.
28 Bellevue Avenue

• Spocott Windmill–About 10 miles west of Cambridge, this classical windmill was built around 1850 and used to grind grain efficiently. There is an old schoolhouse, a tiny cottage, and a well nearby. Worth an Uber drive.
Phone: 410-228-7090
Rt. 343 Between Richardson Road and Castle Haven Road

EATERIES

• Bistro Poplar–French Cuisine
Phone: 410-228-4884
535 Poplar Street

• Canvasback Restaurant Irish Pub–Irish along with French and Italian choices.
Phone: 410- 221-7888
422 Race Street

• Don Chuy Mexican Taqueria
Phone: 410-228-2969
411 Academy Street

place among the great heroines of American heritage.
Phone: 410-228-0401
424 Race Street

• Choptank River Lighthouse at Eaton Point. Across from the Yacht Club: a reproduction of the screw-pile lighthouse that years ago sat at the mouth of the Choptank River. Free to walk through. This is part of Governor's Hall at Sailwinds Public Park.
Phone: 410-463-2653
1 High Street

- **Jimmie & Sooks**–Named after the male crab (Jimmies) and female crab (Sooks).
  Phone: 410-228-0008
  527 Poplar Street

- **Ava's Pizzeria**–We enjoyed a great pizza here.
  Phone: 443-205-4350
  534 Poplar Street

- **The Wine Bar & Shop**–They serve select local wines, and artisan cheeses from around the world, along with chocolates.
  Phone: 410-253-9248
  414 Race Street

- **Snapper Waterfront Café**–Watch the local watermen in the scenic Cambridge Creek while enjoying Caribbean and Maryland inspired cuisine on the deck.
  Phone: 410-228-0112
  112 Commerce Street

- **Carmela's Cucina**–A taste of Italy in the heart of the Chesapeake. They serve family-style Italian meals.
  Phone: 410-221-8082
  400 Academy Street

- **Blue Point Provision Company**–At the Hyatt Regency Hotel.
  Phone: 410-901-6410
  100 Heron Blvd.

We stayed at the Cambridge Yacht Club for two nights.

NEXT DESTINATION: OXFORD, MARYLAND - 10 Miles

Oxford is a tiny, charming town, well-known by boaters who travel the Bay. Its slow pace of life and beauty make it a favorite weekend spot for all yachtsmen. It is only 10 miles from Cambridge, but it is worth a visit for at least one night.

Retrace your steps entering Cambridge and follow the marks out the Choptank River to the 35-foot Choptank Light. Bear to starboard at 18 degrees to Red Buoy "2" at the entrance to the beautiful Tred Avon River. You have arrived at the historic town of Oxford. On the point to starboard is the Tred Avon Yacht Club.

Since it took less than an hour to get to Oxford, you may want to take a few hours to explore the Tred Avon and its branches. The River and its tributaries are deep and well-marked. You will be treated to spectacular views of beautiful homes on both sides. Get your binoculars ready.

Chapter 16
Oxford, Maryland
HISTORY

The city of Oxford was officially founded by the Maryland Legislature in 1683, making it one of the oldest towns in Maryland. Along with the city of Annapolis (known as Anne Arundel then), Oxford was specifically designated as a seaport. The town became very prosperous and was known for its tobacco exporting, with the British being the most important customer. Oxford's most famous citizen was Robert Morris, Jr, the son of a wealthy Liverpool shipping agent. When the senior Morris died, his son inherited most of his considerable wealth at the young age of sixteen. The son learned quickly and parlayed the inheritance into even greater wealth. He became interested in politics and was an important Founding Father. Once the Revolutionary War commenced, Robert Morris was placed in charge of finances and contributed his personal monies to purchase arms and ammunition for the cause.

Robert Morris was the only Founding Father who signed the Articles of Confederation, the Declaration of Independence, and the Constitution. Unfortunately, later in life, during an economic panic, he went bankrupt and served several years in debtors' prison.

After the Revolutionary War ended, the town of Oxford came upon challenging times when the British ceased tobacco imports. Later, when oysters became a popular food, Oxford was able to get a railroad spur that aided the town with its large shipments of oysters around the country. But when oysters were over-harvested, Oxford again declined economically. Now the town is known for its fine boatyards, crabbing, and tourism.

ARRIVAL BY WATER

Once you have finished puttering up and down the lovely Tred Avon River and its branches you can make your way back to Town Creek, the waterway in the center of Oxford. The Town Creek channel is said to have at least a five-foot depth through its entire course.

OVERNIGHT

- **Safe Harbor Marina**—We recommend a stay at Safe Harbor Marina (formerly Brewer Oxford Boat Yard and Marina) which is on the immediate right before you enter Town Creek. They have gas, diesel, and 90 slips for boats up to 60'. Amenities include an elevated pool, bicycle rentals, and a Ship's Store. Also available at your slip are Wi-Fi, pump-out, shore power, and fresh water hookups. The marina is a full-service facility that is equipped to handle most repairs. Everything in Oxford is within walking distance. *Phone: 410-226-5101*

SIGHTS

- **Robert Morris Inn**-Established in 1710, it is the oldest full-service Inn in America. Robert Morris died here in Room #1. Some believe his ghost still roams around the Inn. Stop here for a cocktail or full dinner.
  Phone: 410-226-5111
  314 N. Morris Street

- **Oxford-Bellevue Ferry**–This historic ferry was established in 1683 making it the oldest private ferry in the US. The tiny ferry boat carries a few cars, bicycles, and tourists. Take a ride over and back just for the fun of it.
  Phone: 410-745-9023
  Bellevue Landing-5536 Bellevue Road
  Oxford Landing-101 East Strand

- **Oxford Museum**–Oxford is the oldest town on the Eastern Shore and one of the oldest in continuous existence in the US. Its first citizens were Choptank Indians. No one knows when the first white settler arrived or who they were, but there were settlers and plantations here as early as 1659. As a town, it preceded both Annapolis and Baltimore.
  Phone: 410-226-0191
  101 Morris Street

- **Mystery Loves Company** is an unusual bookstore and remains the only store specializing in new and gently used mysteries in the Baltimore-Washington area and from New Jersey to Florida. This is the bookshop for Scribes of the Shore.
  Phone: 410-226-0010
  202 S. Morris Street

The Oxford Bellevue Ferry underway

With our short trip from Cambridge and time to explore after tie-up, we elected to stay in Oxford for one night. Be sure to take a stroll along the beautiful streets of this quiet and lovely Eastern Shore town.

EATERIES

- **Robert Morris Inn**–They have a great menu with excellent crab cakes.
  Phone: 410-226-5111
  314 N. Morris Street

- **Pope's Tavern**–This cute tavern is located in a lovely B&B and is known for its fine food.
  Phone: 410-226-5220
  504 S. Morris Street

- **Latitude 38**–Lovely bistro, excellent menu, about a mile walk from the marina. We had a delicious dinner here.
  Phone: 410-226-5303
  26342 Oxford Road

NEXT DESTINATION: ST. MICHAELS, MARYLAND - 28 Miles

Departing Oxford is a bit different from your arrival into the Choptank River if you are heading north, which we were. Although St. Michaels is only seven miles away by land using the Oxford Bellevue Ferry, it is a long way around by sea; some 28 miles if you take a shortcut.

The shortcut by sea involves cruising through Knapps Narrows, which we did. Head south out of the Tred Avon toward the Choptank River Light and turn to starboard on a course of 307 degrees for 7.3 miles. This will take you to the entrance of Knapps Narrows. There is a bascule bridge over the channel with a vertical clearance of 12 feet. The bridge will open upon request by calling on Ch. 13.

In the spring of 2018, the Army Corps of Engineers dredged the length of Knapps Narrows to 9 feet at mean low water.

After the picturesque cruise through the Narrows there is a choice. For shallow draft vessels, one can turn north to 354 degrees when past Green "1." There are shallows in this area, so proceed with caution. When arriving at Green Can "3" modify your course to 15 degrees. Proceed past Red "4" and Green "5" and a series of mooring buoys near Poplar Island. There is currently (summer of 2020) work being done on Poplar Island to rebuild its land mass. There may be barges and cranes in the vicinity. Cruise past Green "5" to Red Nun "8" at the entrance to Eastern Bay and then a new course of 42 degrees for four miles to Red Buoy "2A." Eastern Bay leads to the Miles River and St. Michaels.

To avoid this narrow and shallow area one can take a course of 303 degrees out of Knapps Narrows. This will take you five miles to Green Buoy "83" in mid-bay. Then turn to starboard to 53 degrees which will take you to the mouth of Eastern Bay and Green "C IE." From here, change course to 76 degrees for 3.4 miles to Red Buoy "2A," the same destination as above.

POINT OF INTEREST

Historically, Poplar Island and the adjacent smaller island were referred to as the Jefferson Islands. These islands were once home to a private club with overnight facilities and a dining room and bar. It was created by a few Democratic Congressmen in 1931 and was known as the Jefferson Island Club. Many Senators, Congressmen, and President Franklin D. Roosevelt went to this hideaway for relaxation and entertainment. A huge party was held there on September 22-23, 1945 to celebrate VJ Day and the end of World War II. Harry Truman enjoyed the Club and played cards there. The demise of the Club occurred after a devastating fire in March 1946. Storms have gradually washed away the shoreline, but now Poplar Island is being reformed with sludge and sand from the deep-water channels of Baltimore Harbor.

Chapter 17
St. Michaels, Maryland

HISTORY

St. Michaels derives its name from the Episcopal Church established there in 1677. The early settlers were involved in tobacco and ship building. Shipwrights were renowned for making fast-sailing schooners, later known as Baltimore Clipper Ships.

During the War of 1812, our old friend, British Admiral George Cockburn targeted St. Michaels to destroy its shipbuilding cap-

ability. On August 10, 1813, his ships raided St. Michaels and bombarded the town. It is rumored that the local residents hung lanterns at night in the woods adjacent to the town center, so the British were deceived into firing into the woods. At least one home was damaged by cannon fire when a cannonball went through the roof and bounded down the stairs. No one was injured and the home is intact. It is a private residence and known even today as the Cannonball House. This is a rare example where a British attack had a minor impact on the town, its population or its shipbuilding industry.

Frederick Douglas was born a slave near St. Michaels. He lived in the town for several years as a youngster until he escaped to freedom. He became a famous abolitionist and writer and returned to St. Michaels only once in later life.

In a pattern we have seen in many small Bay towns, as the tobacco or shipbuilding industry faded, the national demand for oysters helped

The "Cannonball House" of St. Michaels, Maryland

The ship fought against the British on Lake Erie during the War of 1812. In 1984 the Meyerhoffs converted the old Inn to a 6-room hotel and restaurant. Sir Bernard Ashley (husband of the fashion designer, Laura Ashley) purchased the property in 1989 and expanded it into a luxury 41 room hotel. Orient-Express Hotels acquired the hotel ten years later and enlarged it to 79 rooms. Orient-Express changed its name to Belmond and the hotel is now known as The Inn at Perry Cabin by Belmond. The original Inn of 1815 remains at the north wing of the manor house. The modem luxurious hotel includes a spa, fine restaurant, pool, and beautiful grounds overlooking St. Michaels harbor.

Scenes from the 2005 movie, The Wedding Crashers, were filmed at the Inn.

ARRIVAL BY WATER

We will pick up on Red "2A" in Eastern Bay where we left off above. Proceed 3.2 miles on a course of 62 degrees to Red Buoy "4." Turn to starboard into the Miles River on a 166 degree course to Red Nun "8," 2.3 miles. Make a slight course adjustment to 164 degrees for 2.2 miles to Red Daymark "12" The River narrows here; follow the Marks to Red Buoy "4" where you bear to starboard toward St. Michaels. As you approach, leave Green Mark "3" to port. The Chesapeake Bay Maritime Museum is straight ahead on your bow with its impressive Hooper Strait Screwpile Lighthouse in the center of the horizon. This is an active museum with many boating and waterman displays. In addition, they have overnight dockage. It is wise to call ahead for reservations, especially on weekends. Members of the museum get priority. They have nice

with the economic revival of these small communities.

Today, St. Michaels thrives on the tourist industry with people often arriving by sea. In the late 1880s, steamboats started coming from Baltimore to St. Michaels to drop off tourists and summer residents. In 1965, the Chesapeake Bay Maritime Museum opened, followed by St. Michaels Harbor Inn, Marina, and Spa, the Crab Claw Restaurant, and The Inn at Perry Cabin.

POINT OF INTEREST

The Inn at Perry Cabin was originally constructed in 1815 by Samuel Hambleton, an aid-de-camp to Commodore Oliver Hazard Perry. It was designed to resemble Commodore Perry's Cabin on his flagship, the USS Niagara.

showers and heads but no fuel or restaurants. There are, however, many restaurants within walking distance.

As you cruise toward St. Michaels watch for "log canoes" which are famous sailing vessels from the area. These originally were used for tonging oysters. They were made with two or three logs hooked together. Once internal combustion engines appeared, the usefulness of these log canoes dwindled. Watermen then began racing the canoes for sport. They are beautiful underway. The log canoes have two tall masts and low freeboards. As many as ten crew members will be onboard and they are often perched out on "hiking boards" to avoid knock-downs. The local Miles River Yacht Club hosts several race days each season, starting in the spring.

OVERNIGHT

In St. Michaels, there are many marinas with slips available for an overnight. The museum has only 20 slips. As members, we usually tie up there. It is a nice spot if you can reserve a slip. It is centrally located and there are many interesting bay-related displays, that are free if you overnight. In addition, there are often teaching activities for the many people exploring the museum and Lighthouse. The pleasant staff can help you with Museum displays and activities.

Also, bicycles are available at no charge.

• **Harbour Inn, Marina, and Spa** is across the harbor, to port as you enter. They have 52 slips for a range of boat lengths. Other amenities include electricity, water, showers, a laundry, and Wi-Fi.
Phone: 410-745-9001 or VHF ch. 16

A view of the St. Michaels Chesapeake Bay Maritime Museum

• **St. Michaels Marina** is also to port with 54 slips, a fuel dock, a small pool, and a restaurant on the premises. Other amenities include a marine store, pump-out, showers, water, electricity, laundry, ice, and Wi-Fi.
Phone: 410-745-2400

• **Higgins Yacht Yard Marina** has 30 slips and no fuel. Amenities of the marina include electric, water, private shower and bathroom facilities, and Wi-Fi.
Phone: 410-924-0452 or VHF ch. 16

St. Michaels is one of the most popular destinations on the Bay and fills up quickly for slips and dinner reservations. It is best to call

Hooper Strait Lighthouse at Chesapeake Bay Maritime Museum at St. Michaels, Maryland.

have about 80 restored bay watercraft including the 1920 Buyboat, *Winnie Estelle*, which is available for tours. Be sure to visit displays in all the buildings, where you often can see boatbuilders at their craft. And don't miss the lighthouse to get a sense of how lonesome and difficult life was for the light keeper.
Phone: 410-745-4962
213 North Talbot Street

• **St. Michaels Winery**–Taste and purchase delicious local wines.
Phone: 410-745-0808
609 S. Talbot Street

• **Classic Motor Museum of St. Michaels**–The exhibits include examples of pre and post-WWII classic automobiles, mid-century muscle cars, vintage trucks, motorcycles, and other era-inspired collectibles. The collections are ever-changing and there is always something new to enjoy.
Phone: 410-745-8979
102 E. Marengo Street

in advance to reserve a slip, especially on weekends. For those who cannot reserve a slip there are several areas nearby for anchoring. And there is a water taxi that can pick you up at your anchorage and drop you off at one of the docks. The water taxi can be reached on VHF Ch.71 or by phone at 410-819-9606

SIGHTS

• **The Chesapeake Bay Maritime Museum**– This active, working museum is located at Navy Point, the former site of seafood packing houses, docks, and workboats. The Hooper Strait Lighthouse was moved to the Museum in 1965 and is the center of attraction as you enter the harbor. The Museum is dedicated to the history of the Bay and its watermen. On their small campus, they

• **St. Michaels Museum** is a local museum in a charming, 19th Century home featuring regional history exhibits and walking tours.
Phone: 410-745-9561
201 E. Chestnut Street

• **Iron Will Woodworks**–They collect and sell treasures from around the country.
Phone: 267-221-5107
114 S. Talbot Street

• **Eastern Shore Brewery**–A fine spot to try a variety of beers (and occasional oysters).
Phone: 410-745-8010
605 S. Talbot Street

EATERIES

- **Bistro St. Michaels**–Delicious French and American food.
  Phone: 410-745-9111
  403 S. Talbot Street

- **208 Talbot**–The name is the address; delicious seafood.
  Phone: 410-745-3838
  208 N. Talbot Street

- **Stars** at the Inn at Perry Cabin. Excellent but pricey, and reservations are required.
  Phone: 410-745-2200
  308 Watkins Lane

- **Harrison's Harbour Lights** at the Harbour Inn Marina and Spa. The upstairs dining room provides panoramic views of the harbor.
  Phone: 410-745-9001
  101 N. Harbor Road

- **St. Michaels Crab & Steak House** is adjacent to St. Michaels Marina. The building that houses the St. Michaels Crab & Steak House dates back to the 1830s when it served as one of St. Michaels earliest oyster shucking sheds.
  Phone: 410-745-3737
  305 Mulberry Street

- **Crab Claw** is next to the Maritime Museum. Steamed hard crabs are available by the bushel, and there is outdoor seating by the water or inside with air conditioning.
  Phone: 410-745-2900
  304 Mill Street

- **Carpenter Street Saloon** is the cornerstone gathering spot for residents, boaters, and tourists.
  Phone: 410-745-5111
  113 S. Talbot Street

- **Crepes by the Sea** serves sweet and savory French crepes for breakfast and lunch. Located on Talbot Street next to Ava's.
  Phone: 410-745-8429
  413 S. Talbot Street

- **Ava's Pizzeria and Wine Bar**–The original with a retractable roof patio and beer tap waterfalls.
  Phone: 410-745-3081
  409 S. Talbot Street

There are many other possible choices for fine Eastern Shore eating.

Enjoy this charming town. It is easy to skip since it is a bit off the main route, but do not miss it. Stay for at least two nights.

NEXT DESTINATION: CHESTERTOWN, MARYLAND - 35 Miles

Retrace your course out of St. Michaels until you at Red Nun "8" in the Miles River 3.6 miles from St. Michaels Harbor. At this point take a course of 9 degrees for 3.5 miles to Green "IP." From there correct to three degrees for 3.2 miles to Green "1K." From here, proceed into Kent Narrows. You will pass under two bridges, the first is a draw bridge with a vertical clearance of 18 feet. This bridge is for local traffic. Call the bridge on channel 13 or 16 to confirm opening times. Be cautious when passing through this bridge. The currents can be very strong; as much as 5-6 knots. If currents are behind you, steerage through the narrow span is challenging. The horizontal clearance is 48 feet, and the bridge is concrete with no tires for protection from striking the concrete sides. It is best to wait for the peak of high tide or trough of low tide and proceed through with no currents. The adjacent bridge is Rt. 50 and has a vertical height of 65 feet.

There are fuel docks on either side of the Narrows and several restaurants on the eastern side. Once through the Narrows follow the marks north through the narrow channel to gain entrance to the Chester River. The channel is said to have four feet of depth at mean low tide, so for deeper draft vessels, pass through at high tide. The channel is narrow, and caution is required if another vessel is approaching. The last Green Day Mark "1KN" is the end of the channel, slowly bear to starboard into the Chester River. Target Green Buoy "9," then two miles to Red Buoy "12" on a course of 58 degrees. Follow the meandering river north for 16 miles to Chestertown with dockage on the western side to port. Incidentally, if you have time, bear to starboard at Red Nun "16" and take a brief cruise up the beautiful Corsica River and check out the lovely homes.

Chapter 18
Chestertown, Maryland
HISTORY

Chestertown is a lovely, historic town of 5,200 residents on the meandering Chester River. It was founded in 1706 and became very prosperous after being named as one of Maryland's six Royal Ports of Entry. The shipping boom that followed made Chestertown the second largest port in the state after Annapolis. Many large and beautiful homes were built along the Chester River during this era.

The reproduction of Sultana docked in Chestertown, Maryland

It is alleged that in May 1774, a few months after the Boston Tea Party, the residents of Chestertown unloaded tea from a British ship, the *Geddes*, in sympathy with their patriot brothers in Boston. It appears this is more of an oral tradition among locals, with little factual support. In any case, each Memorial Day Weekend, the locals have an elaborate reenactment in town and on the docks with men dressed in the uniforms of the day.

Another British Navy schooner, "*HMS Sultana*," patrolled the Colonial coastline from 1768 to 1772 to collect duties and frustrate smuggling. In 2001, a reproduction of this vessel was built in Chestertown and is part of the "Tea Party Festival" each year. This replica also sails to ports around the Bay on Goodwill Tours. She has two masts and a prominent black and orange/yellow hull that can easily be identified on the water. We saw her tied up at Alexandria, Virginia when we cruised to Washington, D.C.

Chestertown is the home of Washington College which was established in 1782. It is the first college chartered in the United States after the American Revolution and the 10th oldest college overall. George Washington lent his name, donated 50 guineas, and served on the First Board of Governors. To this day, it has remained a small liberal arts college with about 1,400 students.

POINT OF INTEREST

One last note of minor historical interest: Dr. William Holland Wilmer was a famous ophthalmologist who established the prestigious Wilmer Eye Clinic at Johns Hopkins Hospital in Baltimore. His father, of the same name, was born in Chestertown. Another Wilmer, Philip G. Wilmer, served as mayor of Chestertown from 1936 to 1963. There is a local waterfront park dedicated to him.

ARRIVAL BY WATER

The trip up the Chester River is lovely in any season, but particularly beautiful in the fall as the foliage presents incredible colors to the cruiser. As you approach Chestertown, about a mile past Red Nun "40" there is only one marina for overnight stays, the Chestertown Marina.

OVERNIGHT

* **Chestertown Marina** is to port. The City has taken over and rebuilt the *Chestertown Marina* with dredging and new floating docks. The other amenities include electric, fuel, pump-out, ice, laundry, bathrooms, Wi-Fi, and winter storage. The staff goes out of their way to help transient boaters.

The town of Chestertown is just a few blocks away.
Phone: 410-778-3616
Email: marina@chestertown.com

The Kitchen Restaurant at the Imperial Hotel in Chestertown, Maryland serving dinner in the street

SIGHTS

* **Washington College**–A short walk will take you to this lovely and historic college.

* **Massoni Art**–There are exhibits of local and national artists on display.
Phone: 410-778-7330
203 High Street

* **Garfield Center for the Arts at the Prince Theatre**–Check their schedule for local entertainment.
Phone: 410-810-2060
210 High Street

- **The White Swan Tavern and B&B**–Stop in for afternoon tea from 3:00-5:00 p.m. at this beautifully restored Inn.
  Phone: 410-778-2300
  231 High Street

Take a walk among the classic Riverfront homes from the 18th and 19th Centuries.

EATERIES

- **Kitchen at the Imperial**–Open for lunch and dinner. When we ate there during the Covid pandemic, they had set tables for service in the street They strongly believe in the farm-to-table (and water-to-table) concept, buying local, supporting their neighbors. The menu changes on a weekly and sometimes daily basis, taking seasonal to a new level and taking advantage of the local bounty provided by the Chesapeake Bay.
  Phone: 410-778-5000
  208 High Street

- **Uncle Charlie's Bistro**–Excellent crab cakes, homemade ice cream and desserts are all available.
  Phone: 410-778-3663
  834B High Street

- **98 Cannon Riverfront Grille**–Good food and a water view. The Grille is located at the Chestertown Marina.
  Phone: 443-282-0055
  98 Cannon Street

- **O'Connor's Irish Pub**–A college tavern for those young at heart.
  Phone: 410-810-3338
  844 High Street

- **China House**–Casual Chinese restaurant with good food.
  Phone: 410-778-3939
  711 Washington Avenue

- **Bad Alfred's**–A unique spot with local craft beers and a distillery that makes Rye, Bourbon, Gin, Vodka, and Brandy along with serving great wood-fired pizzas. Fun spot.
  Phone: 443-282-0163
  323 High Street

We elected to stay for two nights and would encourage you to do the same.

NEXT DESTINATION: ROCK HALL, MARYLAND - 37 Miles

Follow your arrival path and proceed down the Chester River to Green "9" our first buoy encountered on our trip up the River. Proceed two miles at 306 degrees to Red buoy "6" then course 345 degrees for two miles to Green Can "3." Turn north at 15 degrees toward Green Buoy "C1." A second Green Can "C3" (note: this can should be honored when coming from the north) is only a half a mile northwest of "C1." From "Cl" a course of two degrees will take you to Red Buoy "4" near the entrance of Rock Hall Harbor.

From this point in our journey, our daily destinations are relatively close together as we enter the Northern Bay which is quite narrow compared to the Southern Bay. So, our time under way will be shorter, which leaves more time to explore our destinations. In quick succession, we will visit Rock Hall, Fairlee Creek, the Sassafras River, the C&D Canal, and Havre de Grace. Rock Hall is across the Bay from our starting point at Baltimore.

Chapter 19
Rock Hall, Maryland
HISTORY

Rock Hall is known as the "Pearl of the Chesapeake." It was settled in 1706 and named after an old mansion made of white sandstones, current whereabouts unknown. In Colonial times, it was a popular port engaged in the trade of tobacco, agricultural products, and seafood. It was also a transit port from Virginia and Southern Maryland for passengers headed to Philadelphia. Such notables as George Washington, Thomas Jefferson, and James Madison made many trips through this small town. Today, it remains a small, but busy port for local commercial watermen. Gratitude was an adjacent town on Swan Creek a short distance northwest, but today it has merged with Rock Hall and is no longer shown on many nautical charts. The town has many shops, restaurants, museums, inns, and 12 marinas, all of which cater to the dominant tourist and boating industry.

Rock Hall, Maryland

ARRIVAL BY WATER

When approaching Rock Hall Harbor pay careful attention to the buoys. I recommend honoring Red Buoy "4" because the depth toward shore is variable. A course of 58 degrees will take you to a Green Can "C1" which I would also honor. We saw a 42-foot yacht aground that did not honor this buoy.

When entering the Rock Hall Harbor, the deeper channel is a large circle that outlines the perimeter. We chose the port side and honored the well-placed daymarks.

OVERNIGHT

We elected to overnight at the Rock Hall Landing Marina.

- **Rock Hall Landing Marina** with its 75 deep water slips is at the far end of the circle at Red "14." In order to accommodate our 61-foot vessel, we tied up at the end of the "T" dock. The floating docks can accommodate vessels up to 120 feet. Their amenities include electric, water, pump-out, pool, clean showers, picnic tables and grills, free bicycles for 1 hour, and laundry facilities. The marina is pet-friendly and the staff is very accommodating. There are several restaurants within walking distance.
  Phone: 410-639-2224
  Email: dockmaster@rockhalllanding.com

- **Osprey Point Inn, Marina, and Restaurant** on Swan Creek is another choice. This marina is located in an area known as The Haven. Bypass Red Buoy "4" at the entrance to Rock Hall Harbor and headed to Green Can "5," then Red "6" into Swan Creek and follow the marks into the narrow channel. Osprey Point Marina is adjacent to Red Mark "4." A prominent home is visible on shore; this is the inn and restaurant. By land, Osprey Point Marina is about a mile from the town center of Rock Hall.

  The marina features 160-slips, floating docks, wide-access channels, full-length finger piers, free Wi-Fi, internet access, water hook-ups, and electric.
  Phone: 410-639-2194
  Email: marina@ospreypoint.com

- **Haven Harbour Marina** is adjacent to Osprey Point Marina on Swan Creek. They are a full-service marina with 200 slips. Amenities include a fuel dock, marine supply store, pool, croquet, bocce ball, horseshoes, and two private swimming pools. Their Passages Restaurant offers dining at a waterfront bar and grill while taking in the panoramic views of Swan Creek.
  Phone: 410-778-6697
  Email: email@havenharbour.com

- **Gratitude Marina** is another marina that is affiliated with Osprey Point Marina and is located nearby, just before turning into Swan Creek. It is the first marina to starboard just beyond Red Day Mark "6." It is a full-service marina with 80 slips. Amenities include a fuel dock, electricity, water bathhouses, and bicycles. Gratitude Marina is within walking distance of Osprey Point Inn.
  Phone: 410-639-7011
  Email: info@gmarina.com

- **Haven Harbor South** (the former Emporium Marina) is located on the southeast portion of Rock Creek Harbor. If you enter Rock Creek Harbor, follow the marks carefully around the periphery, as noted. We have stayed at this marina in the past and it is a nice facility.

  Haven Harbour South is a full-service marina with 150 slips. Amenities include a pool and marine store, but no fuel. At the Admirals Club Beachside Bar (open on weekends only) you can enjoy food and drink while taking in panoramic views of Rock Hall Harbor.
  Phone: 410-778-6697
  Email: email@havenharbour.com

Weekends are busy in Rock Hall with transient boaters, so reservations at any marina are recommended. We elected to stay for one night.

SIGHTS

Rock Hall has one of the best websites of the small towns we visited. Check it out:

www.rockhallmd.com

- **Osprey Point Inn**–They have a lovely Restaurant in a Colonial-style waterfront home. There is a nice bar and one of the best

Osprey Point Restaurant, Rock Hall, Maryland

restaurants in Kent County. Their adjacent marina has all the required amenities.

Phone: 410-639-2194
20786 Rock Hall Avenue

- **Mainstay**–The Mainstay programs are a diverse offering of concerts by local, regional, national, and international musicians. Offering 100+ concerts each year, the Mainstay is especially proud of its reputation for jazz excellence dating back to our early association with jazz great Charlie Byrd. Check their website for shows.

Phone: 410-639-9133
5753 Main Street

- **Pirates and Wenches Fantasy Weekend**–Fun activities for a weekend in August. Check **www.rockhallmd.com** for dates.

ARTS

There are many art shops in town. Again, check the Rock Hall website for a list.

EATERIES

- **Osprey Point Restaurant**–As noted above it has excellent cuisine and ambiance. Open Wednesday-Sunday for dinner only.

Phone: 410-639-2194
20786 Rock Hall Avenue

- **Passages Bar & Grill**–Great views at Haven Harbor Marina on Swan Creek.
  Phone: 410-778-6697
  20880 Rock Hall Avenue
- **Harbor Shack**–Local fare with music on weekends. Open Thursday through Sunday.
  Phone: 410-639-9996
  20895 Bayside Avenue

- **Waterman's Crab House**–A restaurant and dock bar on the harbor with great sunsets and crabs galore. Open every day for lunch & dinner.
  Phone: 410-639-2261
  At the foot of Sharp Street

There are many other great restaurants. The best source is **www.rockhallmd.com**.

NEXT DESTINATION: FAIRLEE CREEK, MARYLAND - 15 Miles

We headed north to Fairlee Creek for our next destination. After retracing our course out of Swan Creek, you must proceed all the way south to Green Can "3" to avoid the 2.5-mile-long Swan Point Bar. Small boats may be seen cutting across this shoal, but if you draw more than 3 feet do not attempt it. You should make a wide turn to starboard around Green Can "3" and target Red Buoy "8" about 3.5 miles away. From here proceed 4.4 miles at 40 degrees to Green Buoy "17." At this point, even though you are very close to shore, the Tolchester Channel is deep, and ships are frequently seen in the narrow channel heading back and forth to the C&D Canal. From a distance, they appear to be running onto shore! From Green Buoy "17" you can run parallel to the channel until Green Buoy "29 " Here, bear to starboard to cross the channel at 75 degrees for 1.5 miles to the entrance of Fairlee Creek.

Chapter 20
Fairlee Creek, Maryland
HISTORY

The most significant historical event in this area took place during the War of 1812. It was known as the Battle of Caulk's Field and it occurred at night on August 30-31, 1814. The Field is about two miles from Fairlee Creek. The British had just burned Washington and were sailing north to attack and destroy Baltimore. They learned that the Americans had militia on the Eastern Shore who were available to aid in the defense of Baltimore. So, as a pre-emptive attack, under Captain Sir Peter Parker (a first cousin of Lord Byron), the British disembarked about 140 troops just south of Fairlee Creek. A local slave informed them where the American militia were stationed. British scouts encountered militia sentries and shots were exchanged. Under the American Lt. Colonel Phillip Reed, who had field experience in the American Revolution, the militia formed a defensive line to take on the British. Reed had 174 men and a few cannons. The British attacked at night under the illumination of a full moon. During the initial onslaught, Captain Parker was seriously wounded in the leg and within a short time, expired from exsanguination. The British removed Parker and retreated to their ships. At that moment, the Americans ran low on ammunition and withdrew to reform a line, but there were no further attacks. The British lost 14 soldiers and 27 were wounded; the Americans had three wounded. This battle gave a moral boost to American forces and revealed to the defenders of Baltimore that the British were not a monolithic juggernaut.

ARRIVAL BY WATER

As you approach Fairlee Creek there is no lighthouse or obvious aid to mark the entrance. It is a bit tricky to navigate in and strict attention must be paid. There are two Green Cans "7" and "9" which, of course, must be kept to port. They are placed parallel to the beach (Shell Point). But as you approach, it appears you must run up on the beach in order to leave the Green Cans to port. So, you head toward the beach and turn sharply to port once you arrive at Green Can "7." You then run parallel to the beach for about 150 yards, then make a 90-degree turn to starboard (before you run up on the next beach straight ahead of you) to enter the Creek. To complicate things, if the tide is going out, there may be a 3-5 knot current pushing you out toward the Bay and there may be considerable boat traffic on weekends. If you have twin screws, throttle your way in. For "first-timers," it is a bit of a challenge.

Caulk's Field Battle Memorial, Fairlee Creek, Maryland

OVERNIGHT

- There are two choices for overnighting on your vessel at Fairlee Creek. First, you can anchor out in the large open creek with 5-foot water depth. The creek is often filled with anchored vessels, so on weekends, plan to arrive early.

- **Mears Great Oak Landing** is the other choice as you enter the creek. You can tie up on the port side They have 350 slips for boats up to 90' and a fuel dock. Amenities include fresh water and electric hookups, pump-out, Wi-Fi, pool, Ship's Store, a Par 3 golf course, and the Waterside Restaurant. We chose to tie up at the marina.
Phone: 410-778-5007 or VHF ch. 9

SIGHTS

- **Shell Point Beach**–Watch the boats pull in and do the parallel run that everyone must do.

A memorial plaque dedicated to those who died at the Battle of Caulk's Field in 1814 at Fairlee Creek, Maryland

EATERIES

• **Mears Great Oak Landing**–Enjoy a casual dinner overlooking Fairlee Creek.
Phone: 410-778-2100
22170 Great Oak Landing Road

• **Jellyfish Joel's Beach Bar** is a Caribbean-like beach bar featuring light food, drinks, and live entertainment complete with palm trees.
Phone: 410-778-5007

GOLF

Unwind on the Par 3, nine-hole golf course that is close to the restaurant.

Fairlee Creek is only 15 miles from Rock Hall by water, so even if you sleep in late you can arrive here before noon. This is a good place to lie on the beach with a cocktail and relax.

NEXT DESTINATION: SASSAFRAS RIVER, GEORGETOWN, MARYLAND - 19 Miles

Head out of Fairlee Creek at 2 degrees toward Red Nun "34A." There are some shallows to starboard. If you have time you may elect to take a short cruise into Worton Creek, just east of the Red Nun "34A." It is a lovely Creek. If you elect to overnight, try the Worton Creek Marina near the head of the creek to port and dine at the Harbor House Restaurant on the hill. To continue to Georgetown, follow the buoys that run parallel with the deep channel. At Red Buoy "48" change course to starboard at 103 degrees and enter the beautiful Sassafras River. Follow the lovely, fresh water (no jellyfish), meandering River to the last mark, Red Nun "14." To port is the town of Fredericktown; a little farther to starboard is Georgetown. Beyond the bascule bridge, there is not much to see unless you want a quiet place to kayak.

Chapter 21

Georgetown (on the Sassafras River), Maryland

HISTORY

We will start with Miss Kitty Knight, a spunky, tall, attractive redhead, who resided in Georgetown on the Sassafras. She came from a prominent local family and was said to have danced with George Washington while he was in Philadelphia at the Continental Convention. She became famous during the War of 1812 when British Admiral George Cockburn attacked and burned Georgetown and Fredericktown (it appears he would have liked to destroy every town on the Bay). Kitty Knight allegedly confronted Cockburn face to face and convinced him not to burn two brick homes in Georgetown, stating she would burn in them if he did. Cockburn was sufficiently impressed with her fortitude, that he spared the homes. The brick structure still stands and is now the Kitty Knight House Inn and Restaurant of Georgetown.

ARRIVAL BY WATER

After turning from the Bay into the Sassafras at Red "48" you can see to starboard the remnants of the popular old resort town of Betterton, now a public beach. In the late 1880s, as steamboat traffic on the Bay increased, considerable tourist traffic came to Betterton from Baltimore and Philadelphia. Here, the

A blue heron watching over the Sassafras River

A plaque honoring Kitty Knight

vessel. We chose to see it by land. See discussion below.

At Red Nun "14" to port is a newer marina, Skipjack Cove Yachting Resort, with over 350 slips, a pool, restaurant (Signals Grille), exercise room, fuel dock, and a 70-ton boat lift along with overnight accommodations for vessels up to 150 feet.

Beyond Red Nun "14" you will see a large marina straight ahead on the north side of the River. This is The Granary Marina, with a well-known restaurant located in the town of Fredericktown.

If you continue another few hundred yards and look straight you will see the large Georgetown Yacht Basin and beyond it on the hill is the famous Kitty Knight House. The Granary and Georgetown Yacht Basin are owned by the same family.

OVERNIGHT

• We elected to stay at the **Georgetown Yacht Basin** for one night. The staff there was very nice and most helpful. GYB has a fuel dock and offers many docking options for vessels 25-90 feet. Some of the many amenities they offer are free Wi-Fi, air-conditioned showers, loaner bicycles, kayaks & pedal boats, picnic area, marine store, pump-out, laundry facilities, pool, propane grills, a beach, and dog walk area.

Note that the tides are substantial on the Sassafras River, measuring up to three feet. Water taxis are available to carry passengers back and forth between the two marinas. We had a wonderful meal at the Kitty Knight

swimming was pleasant because the fresh water of the Sassafras River kept jellyfish away. Piers and hotels were built, and the town became a busy beach resort. The town fell upon hard times during the depression. In 1952, with the completion of the Chesapeake Bay Bridge, Betterton further deteriorated. Kent County took over the property and built a boardwalk, bath houses, and a pavilion in 1976. The clean, quiet, freshwater beach is open to the public.

Continue east up the beautiful, winding Sassafras River and follow the marks and buoys. Be careful to honor the green marks on the port side, for there are shallows close by. As you pass Red Nun "6" look north into Back Creek to see on a distant hillock the classic Georgian Mansion known as Mount Harmon Plantation. This beautifully restored property is open for tours. There is a pier to access the Plantation, but it will accommodate only up to a 30-foot

House and took a tour of the first floor of the Inn after our meal.

We were pleased that the Georgetown Yacht Basin offered a complimentary car for use of its patrons. We took advantage of this to drive to the Mount Harmon Plantation.

Waypoint: 39° 21.66 N / 75° 53.08 W
Phone: 410-648-5112
Email: info@gybinc.com

POINT OF INTEREST

- **Mount Harmon Plantation**–We went to see the Mount Harmon Plantation by land. It is about six miles from the Granary by car. It was built in 1730 and is a classic example of a traditional Tidewater tobacco plantation from that era. Today it is on the National Register of Historic Places. Over the years the ownership has changed hands, but recently considerable sums were spent by members of the DuPont family to restore the Plantation to its original grandeur. It is open to the public for certain hours. In addition to the amazing Manor House, be sure to walk around the Gardens and Nature Trail. This Plantation is worth seeing.

Phone: 410-275-8819
600 Mount Harmon Road

SIGHTS

- **Kitty Knight House Inn and Restaurant**–Any overnight stop in Georgetown must be accompanied by a lunch or dinner here. The view down the Sassafras is quite spectacular. You should roam around the building and the grounds.

Phone: 410-648-5200
14028 Augustine Herman Highway

- **Town of Galena**–It is a small crossroads about two miles south. Galena is the name for a lead ore deposit that resembles silver. It's possible there was a mine here in Colonial times. The town is a cute crossroads with antique shops and stores.

EATERIES

- **Kitty Knight House**–See above. Reservations are strongly recommended.

The Mount Harmon Plantation of Georgetown, Maryland

- **Signals Grille and Deck** is located at the Skipjack Cove Yachting Center. You can dine inside the restaurant or outside on the deck overlooking the Sassafras River.
Phone: 410-275-2122
150 Skipjack Road

- **The Jefas Mexican Grill** is located in Galena. They serve authentic Mexican food, and lots of it.
Phone: 410-648-7182
100 West Cross Street

NEXT DESTINATION: BACK CREEK AND THE C & D CANAL, MARYLAND - 23 Miles

We next proceeded to Back Creek (C&D Canal) and stayed overnight at the Schaffer's Canal House on the north side of the Canal. The C&D Canal is a busy thoroughfare with large ships coursing its waters day and night. Also, there are many currents and eddies swirling in the canal; stay alert.

Chapter 22

Chesapeake City and the C&D Canal (Back Creek), Maryland

HISTORY

Chesapeake City is about evenly divided on the north and south sides of the C&D Canal. The town was originally called Bohemia Village, named around 1661 by an early resident, Augustine Herman. Herman was born in Prague, Czechoslovakia and moved to America as a surveyor and cartographer.

"Time Out" docked at Schaefer's Canal House of Chesapeake City, Maryland

He was hired by Cecil Calvert to make a map of the Chesapeake and Delaware Bays. As a reward, he was granted 4,000 acres of land in what is now part of Cecil County. Herman wrote about creating a canal between the upper Bay and the Delaware River, but for various reasons, no action was taken. It was not until 1824 that political and financial events came together, and the construction of the canal began with 2,600 laborers. They utilized hand tools and horses to dig out the 14-mile-long canal. When completed in 1829 it was 10 feet deep and 66 feet wide with several locks. Mules were used to pull vessels back and forth. The canal split the town into halves and in 1839 the name was changed from Bohemia Village to Chesapeake City.

The Old Lock Pump House was added in 1837 to move water on either side of the locks. It used two steam engines to power the pumps that consisted of a 39-foot wheel. This huge device could move 20,000 gallons of water per minute.

the US with over 15,000 vessels passing through each year. It can accommodate vessels up to 900 feet in length and the bridge has a clearance of 140 feet.

As of the 2010 census, there are 670 residents of Chesapeake City.

The Chesapeake Bay Pilots keep an overnight facility on the north side where they can rest before and after their piloting work.

ARRIVAL BY WATER

We will retrace our course out the Sassafras and head north toward the Elk River. Look for Red Buoy "2" which marks the right side of the deep channel at the northern mouth of the Sassafras. Always beware of ship traffic and remember that they often travel at 15+ knots. We took a course of 55 degrees and ran just outside the channel parallel with the red buoys. Shortly after heading northeast, you will see the lovely Turkey Point Lighthouse high on a bluff to port. It is one of the Chesapeake's original 74 lighthouses and was completed in 1833. The bluff is about 100 feet above the water and the lighthouse adds another 35 feet. The last lighthouse keeper was a woman, who retired in 1947 when the light was automated.

POINT OF INTEREST

One brief historical sidelight here. The Elk River played a minor role during the American Revolution. British General Howe planned to attack and occupy Philadelphia. He sailed up the Bay and discharged 15,000 British troops along the Elk River in Cecil County on August 27, 1777. This invasion more than doubled the population of the entire County! There were

The Chesapeake and Delaware (C&D) Canal Bridge at Chesapeake City, Maryland

This complex is a National Historic Landmark and is open to the public as a museum on the south side of the canal.

By 1927, the locks were removed, and sea level was equalized with the depth increased to 35 feet and the width to 450 feet. A vertical lift bridge was built to connect north and south Chesapeake City. But on July 28, 1942, the bridge was completely destroyed when a ship struck it. The new bridge was completed in 1949.

The Canal is now owned by the Federal Government and is today, the busiest canal in no battles, and the British marched this huge army to occupy Philadelphia.

Then again, during the War of 1812, our "old friend," Admiral Cockburn, attempted to sail up the Elk River and burn Elkton. The local militia held him off and he departed for his next port of destruction, Havre de Grace, and our penultimate port of call.

As we continue up the Elk River, next on the starboard side is the mouth of the lovely Bohemia River at Red Buoy "14." This is an alternative stop for the night if you want a quiet evening. We recommend the Bohemia Bay Yacht Harbour.

- **Bohemia Bay Yacht Harbour** has slips for over 300 boats. Amenities include gas and diesel, laundry rooms, bathrooms and showers, Wi-Fi, free cable TV, pool, a Marine Store, and shaded picnic areas with tables. Their Yacht Shop can provide a variety of marine services They have a 50 metric ton Marine Travelift and can handle most general, plumbing, and engine repairs.
Waypoint: 39° 29.1' N, 75° 53.5° W
Phone: 410-885-2601

We, however, proceeded to the C&D Canal, following the daymarks into Back Creek. When there are no more daymarks, you are in the Canal. Stay in the middle except to give a wide berth to ships. And watch behind you.

OVERNIGHT

- We docked at **Schaefer's Canal House** on the north side of the Canal just beyond the bridge. There are 35 slips at the marina, with a fuel dock and a nice restaurant and bar. A small ferry is available to take passengers across the canal to the south side and the center of town, with its cute homes and shops. The C&D Canal Museum is also nearby but was closed during our visit. While docked here you can watch the tugs and ships course through the Canal within throwing distance.

- Alternative dockage is on the south side of the Canal at the **Chesapeake Inn and Marina** just beyond the bridge. They have 60 slips, with a nice restau-

A tugboat churning through the C&D Canal at Chesapeake City, Maryland

rant and bar along with an Inn for overnight guests. The marina is located in a small cove that is protected from the currents and eddies of the canal.

Phone: 410-885-2040
Email: dockmaster@chesapeakeinn.com

Whichever marina you choose, consider staying for two nights.

SIGHTS

- **C&D Canal Museum with Old Lock Pump House**–This is free and worth a visit. Included is a replica of the Bethel Bridge Lighthouse and the history of the pumping mechanism to control water flow through the locks. Unfortunately, it was closed during our visit.
  Phone: 410-885-5622
  815 Bethel Street

- **Bayard House**–The oldest building in Chesapeake City from c. 1780. The building is now a restaurant.
  Phone: 410-885-5040
  11 Bohemia Avenue

- **Doc Smithers B&B**–Stop by for noon tea or an evening ice cream social.
  Phone: 410-885-3820
  204 Bohemia Avenue

- **Chesapeake City Ferry Service**–Take the 5-minute ferry ride between the north and south parts of the city that carries passengers and bicycles only — no cars.
  Phone: 443-566-3386
  1 Bohemia Avenue

EATERIES

- **Chesapeake Inn**–Fine food at the marina with a view from the south side.
  Phone: 410-885-2040
  605 Second Street

- **Tap Room Crab House**–This is the place on the south side for locals, boaters, and crab lovers. Included on the menu are Maryland steamed blue crabs, other seafood items, and Italian fare.
  Phone: 410-885-2344
  210 Bohemia Avenue

- **Bayard House Restaurant**–Includes Hole in the Wall Pub, and the Canal Eagle Umbrella Bar with a fine chef. It is the oldest building on the south side of town.
  Phone: 410-885-5040
  11 Bohemia Avenue

- **Schaefer's Canal House**–Wonderful food on the north side with a view. They have weekday specials from 4:30 p.m. till close and daily specials from 11:00 a.m. till close
  Phone: 410-885-7200
  208 Bank Street

NEXT DESTINATION: HAVRE DE GRACE, MARYLAND - 19 Miles

Retrace your course out of the Canal and Back Creek to the Elk River. We suggest running parallel to the Green Marks in the Elk River Channel heading southwest. As you pass Turkey Point look for Green/Red Can "ER" and leave it to starboard. From high above, Turkey Point light looks down on you as you head west toward Red / Green Buoy "A." From there, head north at 345 degrees to Green Buoy "1S," then follow the narrow channel marks for 5.5 miles to Havre de Grace on the port side. The town of Perryville is on the starboard side of the Susquehanna as you approach.

Chapter 23
Havre de Grace, Maryland
HISTORY

In Colonial times, Havre de Grace was known as Susquehanna Lower Ferry, until the name was changed in 1785. The new French name, that means "Harbor of Grace" was suggested by Marquis de Lafayette because the town reminded him of the seaport, Le Havre, on the northern coast of France. Today, the locals have dropped any suggestion of a French pronunciation and the town is known as "Have-er-de-grace." With a population of about 12,900, Havre de Grace was designated as one of the "20 Best Towns in the US" by Smithsonian Magazine in 2014.

The Colonial Continental Congress seriously considered designating Havre de Grace as the Capital of the new nation. The proposal lost by 1 vote. Instead, a swamp on the Potomac became our Capital, Washington, D.C.

Our old nemesis, British Admiral Cockburn, made life miserable for Havre de Grace during the War of 1812 when he attacked and burned the town during the first week of May 1813. Cockburn then sent British troops about one mile north to Principio Furnace to destroy the important iron foundry where cannons were manufactured for the US Army and Navy. The information and directions were given to the British by a local resident who sympathized with the enemy.

From Havre de Grace, the British sailed to the Eastern Shore to burn Fredericktown and Georgetown on the Sassafras, as noted in Chapter 21.

During the Civil War, there was no combat in the Havre de Grace region. However, the town served as a stopping off point for the Underground Railroad that aided fugitive slaves traveling to Philadelphia.

From 1912 to 1950, the popular Havre de Grace Racetrack hosted many horse races and included such famous horses as Seabiscuit, Man O' War, Citation, and others.

The Concord Point Light, built in 1827, is the oldest continuously operating lighthouse in Maryland and is easily seen as one approaches the town. As noted on the plaque on page 115, Mr. John O'Neill was one of the few residents of Havre de Grace who fired back at the British invaders in 1813 and became a local hero.

Just south of Havre de Grace is the town of Aberdeen and its adjacent US Army Base, Aberdeen Proving Ground, where weapons and tactics are tested. Don't be surprised if you hear loud booming from time to time.

The famous baseball player for the Baltimore Orioles, Cal Ripkin, was born in Havre de Grace.

ARRIVAL BY WATER

As you approach the town, honor the Green Buoy "17." There is plenty of deep water as you arrive at the marinas along the edge of the town. We saw no need to go beyond the railroad bridge that has 52 feet of vertical clearance.

OVERNIGHT

• There are several marinas along the town of Havre de Grace. We chose **Tidewater Marina** with its 160 protected slips. This is a working marina with pull-out facilities, fuel docks, and a marine store. Call ahead a day or two before your arrival date to make reservations. We were directed into a narrow fairway just beyond the 'Willow Tree.' The entrance was no more than 60 feet wide. Use caution in windy conditions. We noted considerable grass growing from the bottom and extending to near the surface in some areas. Our props were not fouled nor were our intakes blocked, but you need to beware. Dredging would clear this but for environmental reasons the state prohibits removal of the grasses. Amenities include bathrooms, Wi-Fi, and picnic areas with grill and tables. *Phone: 410-939-0951*

SIGHTS

• **Havre de Grace Maritime Museum**–Their mission is to collect, document, preserve, and interpret the maritime skills and cultural heritage of the Lower Susquehanna River and Upper Chesapeake Bay region.
Phone: 410-939-4800
100 Lafayette Street

• **Decoy Museum**–Established in 1986, the museum houses one of the finest collections of working and decorative Chesapeake Bay decoys ever assembled.
Phone: 410-939-3739
215 Giles Street

• **Opera House and Cultural Center**–The Cultural Center at the Opera House embodies the community's commitment to the arts, the preservation of local history, and access to a state-of-the-art facility that is accessible to all.
Phone: 443-502-2005
121 N. Union Avenue

• **Bulle Rock Golf Course**–Three miles south of town. For golfers interested in seeing the

Concord Point Lighthouse at Havre de Grace, Maryland

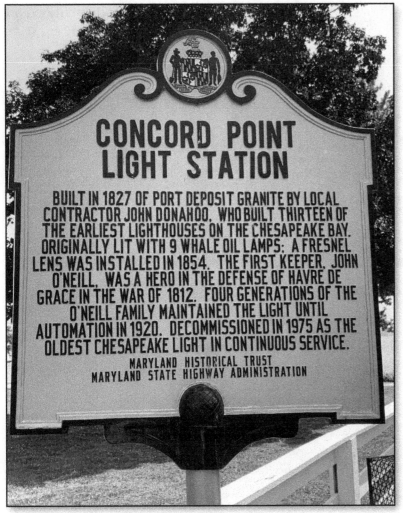

A brief history of Concord Point Light at Havre de Grace, Maryland

• **Tidewater Grille**–Great seafood and a fine menu. Extensive use of glass and the open design ensures views of the water regardless of where you sit. Fresh seafood and local fare are menu mainstays. Live entertainment on Friday and Saturday evenings featuring jazz, classic rock, and 'Americana'.
Phone: 410-939-3313
300 Franklin Street

• **MacGregor**–Very good seafood, wonderful deserts, near the water. On Sundays, the tavern features their Build-Your-Own Bloody Mary Bar.
Phone: 410-939-3003
331 St. Johns Street

• **La Cucina**–Very good authentic Italian. The menu offers pizza, subs, and Italian entrees. We had an excellent dinner here.
Phone: 410- 939 1401
103 N. Washington Street

• **Backfin Blues: Creole De Graw**–Cajun and Creole, seafood, near the waterfront. Great for Sunday brunch and Live Entertainment Thursdays. Closed Monday & Tuesday.
Phone: 443-502-8191
400 N. Union Avenue

• **Bomboy's Home Made Ice Cream**–The real stuff, delish, and homemade chocolates too.
Phone: 410-939-2924
329 Market Street

course or playing here, this course was rated #1 in Maryland by Golf Digest.
Phone: 410-939-8887
320 Blenheim Lane

• **Havre de Grace Seaplane Base** is located just before the railroad bridge. If you want to see the area from a plane, here is your chance.
Phone: 410-942-1444
309 St. John Street

NEXT DESTINATION: BALTIMORE, MARYLAND - 43 Miles

Follow your course out of Havre de Grace to Red Green Buoy "A," then south at 206 degrees 2.7 miles to Green Buoy "3" at the edge of the deep channel. Relating to the Aberdeen Proving Ground there is a Restricted Area here along the Western Shore from Spesutie Island to Pooles Island, then into Middle River. Also, there are many buoys in this area of the Bay that requires full attention and caution. Therefore, we followed the deep Channel Marks into the Patapsco River as follows:

Green Buoy "IER" then 256 degrees, 1.2 miles to

Green Buoy "49" continue 256 degrees, 1.3 miles to

Green Buoy "47" continue 256 degrees, 1.2 miles to

Green Buoy "45" change course to 241 degrees, (cross the channel), miles to

Red Buoy "38 A" change course to 222 degrees, 1.9 miles to

Red Nun "34 A " change course to 234 degrees, 1.6 miles to

Green Buoy "9" change course to 248 degrees, 2.3 miles to

Pooles Island Bar Beacon, change course to 242 degrees (pass Red Buoy "4" & "2"), 7.0 miles to

Lower Range Front Light, change course to 278 degrees, 2.9 miles to

Red Buoy "6" then follow the Brewerton Channel 9 miles into Baltimore's Inner Harbor.

Some boaters may want to visit Middle River. There are many marinas and restaurants there. As discussed under the Baltimore History section, the Glenn L. Martin Airport is located at the origin of Middle River. There is a fascinating aviation museum located there that is worth seeing.

Chapter 24
Summary and Conclusions

We have returned to our starting point at the Baltimore Inner Harbor. We visited 23 ports of call and covered over 1,200 miles in about forty days. Our time was well-invested visiting Maryland, Virginia, and Washington, D.C. We have discovered much about this magnificent estuary, the Chesapeake Bay. We have learned about its fascinating history and the contributions to our nation from the people and places around the Bay. After an experience like this one, you cannot help but respect all those who stood before us, made crucial decisions, traveled under great duress, and, in many cases, fought and died for principles they held dear. Our exploration touched on many of these important stories. There are more to be told. But perhaps we got a glance, a framework, a point of discovery to lead to more reading and research. One can imagine the great men of our founding; Washington dining in Annapolis, resigning his commission in the State House, traveling by boat to disembark at Rock Hall on the way to Philadelphia; or trekking to Yorktown to surround Cornwallis; Jefferson residing in Annapolis, perhaps at Middleton's Tavern, discussing the momentous issues of the day; Franklin, Madison, and Hamilton traveling by boat; presumably in danger from the British fleet roaming about the Bay; the four Maryland signers of the Declaration of Independence at soirees discussing unjust British taxation; the many ordinary men and women who paid attention to the great issues swirling around our country's founding; and the distraught men who stood next to Washington in bare feet; fighting and dying for the idea of freedom.

Is it not fascinating that, unlike other revolutions in history, the American Revolution was carried out by the wealthy aristocracy? And once the objective was achieved, these same aristocrats, from a blank sheet, created a new form of government with a primary goal of freedom for all men. And the same document gave citizens the right to choose their leaders and to create a central government with three parts to keep it from becoming too powerful and ultimately designed to leave its population in peace. George Washington is quoted as saying, "Government is not reason; it is not eloquence; it is force! Like fire, it is a dangerous servant and a fearful master."

One final thought regarding the history of the Bay area. As I have studied the historical events that have taken place in and around the Chesapeake Bay, it has occurred to me that there are few places that have had such an impact on world history. That may sound like a slightly outrageous claim, but let's look at it.

Certainly, the Mediterranean Sea would rate very high in historical significance. Most of the ancient Western civilizations had their origins and growth there. Significant sea battles, like Salamis during the Greek-Persian Wars occurred in the Mediterranean Sea. The Battle of Actium, when the Roman Civil War was decided against Mark Antony and Cleopatra and in favor of Augustus Caesar was off the coast of Greece. On October 7, 1571, at the Battle of Lepanto, the Muslims were defeated by a navy of Christian nations. This battle had a huge impact on world history. Many naval battles were fought in the Mediterranean Sea during both World Wars.

London and the English Channel would also rate very high in historical significance. England was invaded by the ancient Romans and in 1066 by William the Conqueror. The D-Day invasion certainly ranks as a world-changing historical event.

The seas of the Western Pacific were sites of many wars among the Asian peoples that affected their histories and ultimately, world history.

But many important and significant historical events have occurred in and around the Chesapeake Bay. Admittedly, these events are of recent origin; since the 1600s. The American Revolution is certainly the most important revolution of modern times. Many key events relating to that Revolution took place in Maryland and Virginia around the Bay. This includes the surrender of Cornwallis at Yorktown.

The War of 1812 largely was played out in the Chesapeake Bay. The powerful British navy acted as if the Bay was its private pond and took liberties up and down its 200-mile extent. The attack on Washington, D.C. and the burning of its public buildings including the nascent Library of Congress, enraged the civilized world, including the British at home. If Baltimore had fallen to the British, would Philadelphia, New York, and Boston have been

next? How would that have altered world history?

During the American Civil War, the Bay played a significant role. The first naval battle of Ironclad ships took place in Hampton Roads, Virginia and caused a permanent change in naval warfare. What if McClellan had been aggressive during his invasion of the Yorktown peninsula and succeeded in capturing Richmond early in the war? What if Lincoln had succeeded in negotiating peace with the South when he sailed from Annapolis to Fort Monroe in Virginia?

Fortunately, there were no attacks in the Chesapeake Bay during either World War, although German U-Boats were active at the mouth of the Bay and sank many commercial ships off the DelMarVa peninsula during World War II. And ironically, the German U-boat, *U-1105* rests at the bottom of the Potomac River after surrendering to the British at the end of the War.

The Naval Base at Norfolk is the largest in the world. The Bay is home to many other military bases and research facilities. It is the home of the Glenn L. Martin aircraft company (now Martin-Marietta) that developed many military aircraft including the largest sea plane and later the first jet sea plane.

Annapolis, Maryland is home to the US Naval Academy. At the Maryland State House in Annapolis, the "first continental congress" met and decided a continental convention was needed to improve on the 13 colonies' interactions after the American Revolution. That Convention, held in Philadelphia, created the greatest document outlining a system of interactions between a government and its people, since the Magna Carta.

And finally, the Bay is the home of Washington, D.C., the most important capital city in the world.

So, when put in historical perspective, at least since 1600, a legitimate argument can be made that the Chesapeake Bay can be ranked in the top five of historically significant areas in world history.

I would be happy to hear other perspectives.

After such a trip as ours, one comes to realize the power of the British Navy during the War of 1812, the "forgotten war." The British took over the Bay for a time and raided and burned so many towns, it is easy to lose count. They operated with no remorse and plundered with little resistance, although there were a few notable exceptions. The Battle of Baltimore gave us our Star-Spangled Banner. And many brave men, including the teens, McComas and Wells, gave their lives to resist the British onslaught. Many Americans died during the Battle of Bladensburg, trying to prevent the British from burning their new Capitol. The nascent American navy was incredibly inadequate, as it was 129 years later at Pearl Harbor. Lessons learned; hopefully.

Our experience was enjoyable and fun. At the same time, however, it was a great learning experience and at times, troubling. Too many Americans have little knowledge of the events and sacrifices of those patriots who created the foundation of freedom we stand on today.

There are many fine, relevant books listed in Appendix A. I am hopeful that readers will find time to read them. I also hope that some readers will attempt to retrace our course through history by visiting some, or all of the ports-of-call on the Chesapeake Bay Odyssey. And there are many other places we did not visit. The study of history is a work in progress. We hope you can join us.

Captain Michael J. Dodd

October 2020

Appendix A-
Additional Recommended Reading

Anderson, E. B. (2009). *Annapolis: A Walk Through History*. Atglen, PA: Schiffer Publishing.

Bailey, P. K. (2011). *Poplar Island: My Memories as a Boy*. CreateSpace.com.

Brennan, D. (1999). *Annapolis: Capital Gateway to Maryland*. Charleston, SC: Arcadia Publishing.

Burdett, H. N. (1975). *Yesteryear in Annapolis*. Ithaca, NY: Cornell Maritime Press.

Chernow, R. (2010). *Washington: A Life*. New York, NY: Penguin Press.

Dodds, R. J. (1995). *Solomons Island & Vicinity*. Solomons, MD: Calvert Maritime Museum.

Doyle, G. (2005). *Gone to Market: The Annapolis Market House, 1698-2005*. Annapolis, MD: The City of Annapolis.

Eshelman, R E., Sheads, S. S., & Hickey, D. R. (2010). *The War of 1812 in the Chesapeake: A Reference Guide to Historic Sites in Maryland, Virginia, and the District of Columbia*. Baltimore, MD: Johns Hopkins University Press.

George, C. T. (2000). *Terror on the Chesapeake: The War of 1812 on the Bay*. Shippensburg, PA: White Mane Publishing.

Healy, D. (2005). *1812-Rediscovering the Chesapeake Bay's Forgotten War*. Rock Hill, SC: Bella Rosa Books.

Horton, T. (1994). *Bay Country*. Baltimore, MD: Johns Hopkins University Press.

Horton, T. (2008). *An Island Out of Time, A Memoir of Smith Island in the Chesapeake*. New York, NY: W.W. Norton & Co.

Jamieson, J. (2009). *Seamanship Secrets: 185 Tips & Techniques for Better Navigation, Cruise Planning, and Boat Handling Under Power or Sail*. New York, NY: International Marine/Ragged Mountain Press.

Klingel, G. (1984). *The Bay*. Baltimore, MD: Johns Hopkins University Press.

Leeland, S. E. (2004). *St. Leonard: A Maryland Tidewater Community*.

Lord, W. (1972). *By the Dawn's Early Light*. New York, NY: W.W. Norton & Co.

Maptech. (2018). *Chesapeake Bay to Florida*. Hilton Head Island, SC: Maptech Embassy Cruising Guides.

Millard, C. (2012). *Destiny of the Republic: A Tale of Madness, Medicine and the Murder of a President*. New York, NY: Anchor Books.

Norris, W. B. (1925). *Annapolis: Its Colonial and Naval Story*. New York, NY: Thomas Y. Crowell Co.

Parks, D. (2008). *Chesapeake Winds and Tides: Journeys among Eastern Shore Islands, Rivers and Communities*. Dover, DE: Cherokee Books.

Parks, R. (1997). *Tangier Island*. Parsons, WV: McClain Printing Co.

Piet, S. & Raithel, A. (2001). *Martin P6M Seamaster: The Story of the Most Advanced Seaplane Ever Produced*. Lawton, OK: Martineer Press.

Robinson, J. D. *America's Privateer, Lynx and the War of 1812*. Newmarket, NH: Lynx Educational Foundation.

Shomette, D. (1991). *Shipwrecks on the Chesapeake*. Centreville, MD: Tidewater Publications.

Shomette, D. (2008). *Pirates on the Chesapeake*. Centreville, MD: Tidewater Publications.

Swanson, J. L. *Manhunt: The 12-day Chase for Lincoln's Killer*. New York, NY: William Morrow Paperbacks.

Washington, G. (2004). *Quotations of George Washington*. Carlisle, MA: Applewood Books.

Appendix B-Recipes

Recipe for steaming hard crabs.

Requirements: a large pot with an elevated grill at the bottom.

Pour in one can of beer and 12 oz of vinegar.

Obtain 1 to 2 dozen live hard crabs.

Begin stacking crabs in the pot in layers using tongs.

Once a layer is in place, generously sprinkle Old Bay Seasoning mixed with Kosher salt, 70/30 on each layer of crabs.

Once all the crabs are loaded and covered with seasoning, place on a hot grill or stove top for 15-20 minutes with a top on tightly.

Remove crabs and place on large picnic table covered with several layers of newspaper or paper bags.

Enjoy with a cold beer.

Recipe for cooking soft crabs

Purchase live soft crabs. At home, clean them by cutting out the eyes and lifting the soft carapace and scraping out the "lungs" or "devil," a circle of pale loose tissue.

Rinse off, then baste in flour, seasoned with a little Kosher salt and black pepper.

Prepare a large frying pan with 50% mixture of olive oil and butter.

Heat until quite hot and put the basted crabs in.

Fry for 5-8 minutes to make them crispy.

Let cool on a towel and eat.

Some prefer eating the soft crab straight away with a knife and fork, but most prefer making a sandwich with lettuce and tomato.

You eat the entire crab, soft shell, legs, and all.

In Maryland, these are considered a delicacy.

Acknowledgments

A journey like this requires considerable help. I thank my wonderful wife and ever first mate, Maureen who not only helped on the boat but has been an excellent editor and proof-reader. Thanks also to Dr. Dave Watt and Rick Sheahan who proofed the book and offered many useful suggestions. We were aided during part of our journey by Dr. Steve Dargan and his wife Carol, along with Dr. John Weigel. Many thanks to them for their help, conversation, and good laughs! In addition, I would like to thank all the people at Seaworthy Publications who helped bring this project to fruition.

Capt. Michael J. Dodd
July 2021

About the Author

Captain Michael J. Dodd grew up in the suburbs of the port city of Baltimore when it was a quiet southern town. His father, Bill Dodd, loved the water and introduced him to boating at a young age. The family often chartered a 38-foot Chris Craft motorboat in the summers to tour the Chesapeake Bay. Michael's father and his older brother would do the navigation and operate the vessel. Captain Dodd recalled, "At age 8, if I was good, I was permitted to steer the boat under direct supervision. I paid attention and learned quickly. We slept onboard nightly under the silence of the clear Bay sky." Captain Dodd never forgot those fond memories.

Over the years he learned to sail and owned several sailboats with partners. He and his wife Maureen also enjoyed chartering power boats with their children and other couples. He eventually accumulated many hours at the helm of various sail and power vessels and decided to test for a US Coast Guard Captain's License. After passing the qualifying exam he was awarded a 50-ton license.

Captain Dodd now owns a 1984 classic 61-foot Hatteras Cockpit Motor Yacht. He and Maureen can handle the boat themselves. It is this vessel, named *Time Out*, that they used to explore the Bay for this odyssey.

You can contact Captain Dodd at: CaptMikeBayOdyssey@gmail.com

Printed in the USA
CPSIA information can be obtained
at www.ICGtesting.com
LVHW011805121023
760795LV00010B/159